Anatoly MARCHENKO

From Tarusa To Siberia

Edited and with
an Introduction by
Joshua Rubinstein

Strathcona

ACKNOWLEDGEMENTS

Joshua Rubinstein, "Anatoly Marchenko: A Life Apart," Copyright © 1977 by Realforms Co., Inc. Reprinted by permission of the publisher.
"The Case of Anatoly Marchenko," tr. Guy Daniels, Copyright © 1975 by Khronika Press. Reprinted by permission of the publisher.
L. Bogoraz and A. Marchenko, "The Invasion of Privacy," Copyright © 1977 by Khronika Press. Reprinted by permission of the publisher.
A. Marchenko, "On the Life of Soviet Workers," tr. Guy Daniels, Copyright © 1978 by Khronika Press. Reprinted by permission of the publisher.

Anatoly Marchenko
From Tarusa to Siberia

CONTENTS

Appendix

FROM TARUSA TO SIBERIA

Pasha and Anatoly Marchenko

INTRODUCTION

Anatoly Marchenko: A Life Apart

Most Soviet dissidents known in the West—Andrei Amalrik, Pavel Litvinov, Andrei Sakharov, Alexander Solzhenitsyn —have belonged to Russia's sophisticated class of scientists and writers. Before they challenged the regime on political issues, they were already concerned with the question of intellectual freedom and censorship in their professional lives. Anatoly Marchenko had different origins.

He was born in 1938, in Barabinsk, a small town in western Siberia. His parents still live in the region, employed as railroad workers; they are both illiterate. Marchenko left school after the eighth grade, two years short of a full secondary education, and went to work on the Novosibirsk hydroelectric station, and then on similar construction projects in Siberia and Kazakhstan. One job was on the Karaganda power station. In his book, *My Testimony*, Marchenko describes what happened to him there:

We young workers lived in a hostel and went dancing at the club. In the same settlement lived some Chechens who had been exiled from the Caucasus. They were terribly embittered: after all, they'd been transported from their homes to this strange Siberia, among a strange and alien people. Between their young people and us constant brawls and punch-ups kept breaking out and sometimes there was a knife fight as well. One day there was a huge brawl in our hostel. When it had all died away of its own accord the police arrived, picked up everyone left in the hostel—the majority of those involved had already run away or gone into hiding—arrested them and put them on trial. I was one of the ones arrested, and they took us away from the settlement, where everyone knew what had happened. They sentenced us all in a single day, with no attempt at finding out who was guilty and who innocent. Thus it was that I found my way to the terrible camps of Karaganda.

Prior to his first arrest, Marchenko had never thought about politics. Even when he worked alongside political prisoners on construction projects, he remained indifferent to their fate. "I used to get my pay, go to dances on my days off and never think a thing of it," he remarks. But his arrest and trial provoked an intense reaction. He felt insulted and degraded. Although the court originally sentenced him to five years in a labor camp the sentence was reduced to two years shortly after it began. Nonetheless, Marchenko was determined to escape not only the camp but the Soviet Union itself. He succeeded in leaving the camp. For a time he lived in Tashkent, getting by with false identity papers. But on October 29, 1960, he and a friend were caught near the Iranian border.

According to *My Testimony*, he was then kept in solitary confinement for five months with no parcels or letters from his family. The KGB accused him of high treason. They cut up his boots "in their search for the plan of a Soviet factory." In return for worthwhile evidence and a confession, they promised him more food. Marchenko refused to cooperate.

His trial began on March 2, 1961, before the Supreme Court of the Soviet Socialist Republic of Turkmenia. It lasted two days. Almost immediately, Marchenko was betrayed. His co-defendant, Anatoly Budrovsky, "had yielded under pressure from the investigator" and gave testimony damaging to Marchenko. The next day, while Budrovsky was convicted of illegally attempting to cross the border and given two years in the camps, Marchenko was found guilty of high treason and sentenced to six years in the labor colonies for political prisoners.

In *My Testimony*, he describes his reaction to the trial:

Once more I was taken back to prison, to my cell. To tell the truth, the length of my sentence made no impression on me. It was only later that each year of imprisonment stretched out into days and hours and it seemed that six years would never come to an end. Much later I also found out that the label of "traitor to the Homeland" had crippled me not for six years but for life. At the time, however, I had only one sensation, and that was that an injustice had been committed, a legalized illegality, and that I was powerless; all I could do was to gather and store my outrage and despair inside me, storing it up until it exploded like an overheated boiler.

I recalled the empty rows of seats in the chamber, the indifferent voices of the judge and prosecutor, the court secretary chewing on a roll the whole time, the silent statues of the guards. Why hadn't they let anyone into the court, not even my mother? Why had no witnesses been called? Why wasn't I given a copy of the sentence? What did they mean: "You can't have a copy of the sentence, it's secret?" A few minutes later a blue paper was pushed through the little trapdoor for food: "Sign this to say that you've been informed of your sentence." I signed it and that was that. The sentence was final, with no right of appeal.

He was then twenty-three years old.

Marchenko spent the next six years in various labor camps and prisons. He suffered irreparable damage to his health; and his contact with other prisoners, most notably with the writer Yuli Daniel, changed the direction of his life. Near the end of Marchenko's term, in 1966, Daniel and Andrei Sinyavsky were defendants in a trial that generated much attention in the West. For several years, both authors had been publishing essays and stories in the West under assumed names. Sinyavsky, especially, under the pseudonym Abram Tertz, had generated much speculation over his true identity: whether or not he was a Jew, a Polish emigre, or, in fact, a Soviet writer. Throughout their trial, the official press denounced Sinyavsky and Daniel. Seeing *Pravda* and other papers, Marchenko and his fellow prisoners at first believed the trial to be a "show trial," with a pair of contrite defendants eager to denounce themselves. Otherwise, they figured, it would take place secretly, with no press coverage or denunciations. But the prisoners after all were experts in these matters, and they soon understood what even the Soviet press could not conceal: that Sinyavsky and Daniel behaved with dignity, that they did not confess, but insisted on their right to freedom of speech. After his conviction, Daniel was sent to the same camp in Mordovia where Marchenko was nearing the end of his six-year term.

When Daniel arrived, Marchenko's work gang arranged for him to join their crew. They knew that Daniel was unaccustomed to hard physical labor. In addition, as they soon learned, an old shoulder wound from the war had not healed properly, making it even harder for Daniel to work. Although Marchenko's crew unloaded timber, they assigned Daniel the easier tasks, like cleaning the wood shed or stacking small logs. Daniel, in turn, developed friendships with several prisoners, including Marchenko. They were both partially deaf and found it amusing to shout in each other's right ear. Daniel understood how Marchenko had matured in the camps, how he had changed from a simple, uncaring worker into a determined and well-informed individual. Daniel wrote to his wife about him and before Marchenko left the camps, Daniel suggested that he visit her—Larisa Bogoraz—in Moscow.

Marchenko went immediately to the capital where he met several of Daniel's friends at the home of Larisa Bogoraz. To them, he resembled a creature from an alien world. While they all knew people who had served terms under Stalin, they believed that under Khrushchev political prisoners had become scarce. And surely, conditions in the camps had improved! Marchenko, in fact, was the first person they had encountered from the camps of the post-Stalin era, and though as Moscow intellectuals they were conscientious seekers of news and information, they soon realized how profound their illusions were. One woman even came to the apartment with a tape recorder, hoping to collect the latest folk songs from the camps.

Marchenko was almost totally deaf, the result of a severe middle ear infection that had proceeded undiagnosed and virtually untreated in the camps. They expected him to eat voraciously, but, as he explained, regardless of his constant hunger, he could eat very little food as his stomach had shrunk from lack of nourishment. Eventually, Marchenko asked for their help. He was determined to write a book about his experiences, to bear witness to the suffering he had seen and endured. They tried to dissuade him. On his first evening in Moscow it was clear to his new friends that he had not seen the last of prison. And later, when his activities brought him further reprisals, the friends who had helped him felt responsible for his fate.

The friends Marchenko made through Larisa Bogoraz were among those most deeply involved in the early stages of the democratic movement. Larisa Bogoraz herself had been a staunch defender of her husband, although by the time of his arrest their marriage had all but formally dissolved. As his wife, she was entitled to maintain personal contact with him while others, mere *friends*, were restricted from doing so. For two more years she would write widely-circulated appeals on behalf of arrested dissidents until, in August 1968, she herself would be arrested in Red Square for demonstrating against the invasion of Czechoslovakia. Marchenko also met Alexander Esenin-Volpin—for many, the father of the democratic movement. A renowned logician and mathematician, Esenin-Volpin had been incarcerated four times in mental institutions in retaliation for his poetry and philosophical essays. It was Esenin-Volpin who first encouraged his fellow dissidents to study Soviet law and it was he who helped to organize the first demonstration on Pushkin Square in support of the Soviet Constitution. (December 5 is celebrated as Constitution Day in the Soviet Union. Since 1965, a small group of people gather in Pushkin Square on that day every year. Usually, they merely stand for a few minutes with their hats off, mutely calling attention to the written standards of law the regime prefers to ignore.)

By making their views known to the authorities, Bogoraz, Esenin-Volpin, and others effected a change in their own lives, which, in turn, transformed the moral climate of Moscow and Leningrad. For years, they had practiced double-think and double-behavior, concealing their ideas on politics and culture from neighbors and colleagues at work. But once they signed appeals to the authorities and to the West, they no longer had something to conceal. Often, their letters and names were broadcast in Russian over Western radio stations, like the Voice of America, the BBC, or Radio Liberty. They became more open—with each other, with casual friends, even with strangers. They overcame their fear and their isolation. At work, colleagues who supported them came forward. Others, who disagreed or feared contact with dissidents, broke off friendships. Even with the KGB, they learned to speak openly of their political and philosophical views. Suddenly, they had cracked the facade of unanimity totalitarian governments impose. For the first time since the early 1930s an independent, more natural social life began to evolve.

Marchenko flourished among these people. Everyone he met seemed to share his compassion and sense of outrage. His friends, though, had to restrain him. In the camps he had studied Lenin, copying passages into a notebook, then exploring their significance for Russia's present situation. Meeting sympathetic people in Moscow, he believed they ought to organize an underground party, secure mimeograph machines, conspire against the authorities.

His friends disabused him of these illusions. The labor camps contained many people who had tried to organize independent circles—study groups—to discuss Marxism and its relation to Soviet society. Invariably, the regime feared the subversive potential of such activity and always imprisoned the participants. In addition, the KGB enjoyed investigating the smallest hints of clandestine activity for they found it psychologically easier to pursue someone who indeed had something to hide.

Marchenko's friends turned to more practical matters. Upon his release, Marchenko had been given a "minus 100," forbidding him to live within a hundred kilometers of certain major cities. He could not stay in Moscow. So his friends helped him find a room in Alexandrov, well outside the capital; he then registered with the police there as he was required to do. He was also supposed to find work but the authorities knew he was sick and did not pressure him to find employment. For long periods Marchenko simply vanished from their sight. Once his friends arranged a month long stay in a Moscow hospital where his ears could be properly treated. At other times he stayed in cottages outside the city, writing his memoir and consulting with friends.

During this time, also, Marchenko and Larisa Bogoraz became lovers. She was nearly ten years older, an intellectual, with advanced degrees in linguistics. For more than a year before they met, she had been involved in political struggle, writing appeals and circulating petitions on behalf of defendants, most notably for her estranged husband, Yuli Daniel. She must have understood, as others did, what lay in store for Marchenko and for herself. They would be married in 1971.

After Marchenko completed writing *My Testimony* in longhand, his friend, Boris Shragin, who came to the West in 1974, volunteered to type it for him. With a second-hand typewriter bought especially for the project, Shragin retreated to his mother's apartment, in a secluded area, where his typing would neither disturb anyone nor arouse suspicion. As usual for such manuscripts, he typed eight copies, pounding heavily on the keys to impress the letters through the layers of carbon. Later, the machine was passed to other dissidents to copy *samizdat* material, until finally the typewriter was confiscated during a search. But even in 1967 the machine was old and the keys worn down. Shragin bruised and cut his fingers so badly that, in the end, he could only copy the manuscript by wearing gloves.

My Testimony was the first account of life in the post-Stalin era prisons and camps of the Soviet Union. It began to circulate unofficially in Moscow, and other books, most notably Valentin Moroz's *A Report from the Beria Reservation* and Edward Kuznetsov's *Prison Diaries*, have since confirmed the incredible, indeed grotesque, episodes Marchenko describes. The chapter headings themselves alert the reader: "Hunger," "Self-Mutilation," "The Man Who Hanged Himself." *My Testimony* makes us believe what we have known all along: that Soviet political prisoners endure systematic starvation, that medical care is perfunctory, that the entire procedure of corrective-labor is designed to humiliate the prisoner, to ruin his health, to break his spirit.

As Marchenko remarks, in camp "you work like an elephant, get fed like a rabbit." The prisoners work long hours, unloading timber, polishing furniture in the camp factory, handling lathes in crowded, noisy rooms. Always there are norms to fulfill, punishments exacted, beatings, weeks in solitary confinement. While Marchenko provides sordid, degrading details of prison life, the collection of human derelicts he encountered leaves the most lasting impression.

Operations for removing tattoos were also very common. I don't know how it is now, but from 1963 to 1965 these operations were fairly primitive: all they did was cut out the offending patch of skin, then draw the edges together and stitch them up. I remember one con who had been operated on three times that way. The first time they had cut out a strip of skin from his forehead with the usual sort of inscription in such cases: "Khrushchev's Slave." The skin was then cobbled together with rough stitches. He was released and again tattooed his forehead: "Slave of the USSR." Again he was taken to hospital and operated on. And again, for a third time, he covered his whole forehead with "Slave of the CPSU." This tattoo was also cut out at the hospital and now, after three operations, the skin was so tightly stretched across his forehead that he could no longer close his eyes. We called him "The

Stare."

Prisoners like this one are actually criminals from the lowest stratum of Soviet society. Imprisoned in camps for violent criminals, they prefer to be transferred to political camps, for they believe the rumors that conditions for "politicals" are better than for ordinary criminals. In fact, the conditions are far worse. So the criminal con employs his own form of protest. Many disfigure their bodies with tattoos. Others rip open their stomachs, swallow sets of dominoes or chess pieces, even bits of glass and barbed wire. "If there had been a museum of objects taken out of stomachs," Marchenko suggests, it would have been the most astonishing collection in the world."

Living among these prisoners and genuine political prisoners, Marchenko underwent a radical, personal transformation. In contrast to other Soviet dissidents, who came to oppose the regime out of an intellectual commitment to truth and justice, Marchenko deliberately cultivated an understanding of the regime only after he sensed his opposition to it. In the camps he read Lenin and Plekhanov for the first time. At lectures he often challenged the "education officers," exposing their false logic and inconsistencies. Provoked by human suffering, he penetrated the facade of lies and hypocrisy that camouflages the Soviet government. *My Testimony* is not an optimistic book. The moral degradation of prisoner and keeper alike is not presented in a manner designed to reinforce one's faith in human nature. Yet Marchenko survived. He did not leave the camps defeated.

Undoubtedly, other former prisoners also wrote about their experiences. Their manuscripts either disappeared or never were completed. But Marchenko had been released at a fortunate time. He found friends who were able to help him. By 1967, there was a widespread network of *samizdat* readers extending beyond Moscow and Leningrad to provincial capitals and even to collective farms. In addition, several dissidents were in close contact with foreign journalists and others who could help transmit material to the West. Gradually, Marchenko became a visible part of this dissident activity. Although his friends had tried to protect him, especially until *My Testimony* was completed, he could not allow them to take all the risks.

When searches took place at the apartment of someone under investigation (or already under arrest), the presence of the KGB discouraged friends and neighbors from visiting the apartment. By law, the police could compel anyone to remain in the apartment for the duration of the search (which could take more than five or six hours), search them also, and include their names in the official protocol of the investigation. This procedure succeeded in isolating the families of dissidents. But the dissidents embarked on a new strategy to embarrass the KGB. When a search took place, friends contacted friends. Then individuals and groups of people would converge on the apartment, demonstrating their solidarity with the family involved.

On September 5, 1967, Marchenko visited the apartment of Lyudmila Ginzburg, whose son, Alexander, was awaiting trial in Moscow. Marchenko came—deliberately—during a search and stayed until its conclusion. His name and address were listed in the official report. In addition, Marchenko signed one of the innumerable appeals that were circulating before the start of Alexander Ginzburg's trial. Demanding an open process, the letter cited violations of law committed by authorities during the investigation. While the accused had been arrested in January he was not brought to trial within nine months, the period stipulated by the Code of Criminal Procedure.

By the winter of 1967-68, the KGB knew about *My Testimony*. But they did not arrest Marchenko, probably because the impending trial of Alexander Ginzburg and Yury Galanskov, who were both well-known publicists, was already generating controversy. The atmosphere was not right for the arrest of another writer. Furthermore, Marchenko's detention would simply lend greater attention to his book. Knowing his character, the KGB realized he would provide another pretext—sooner or later—for his own arrest. They were not mistaken. Still, for nearly half a year, Marchenko endured continual harassment. In February, Larisa Bogoraz complained to the authorities "about the grossly illegal methods of persecution practised in the case of former political prisoner Anatoly Marchenko." As she later described in an open letter to the West, Marchenko's life was growing considerably more difficult:

> His book . . . aroused such hatred for him in the KGB that they began to bait him like a hare: KGB agents followed on his heels for months on end—I've spotted them so often that I know many of them by sight. And not only in Moscow, where he worked, and Aleksandrov where he lived: he went to visit relatives in Ryazan but wasn't allowed to leave the train and had to return to Moscow. He was seized on the street almost as soon as he had been discharged from hospital; and they smashed his face in and shoved him into a car when he came to Moscow for a literary evening.

Despite such conditions, Marchenko increased his activities. In March 1968, Alexander Chakovsky, the editor of *Literaturnaya Gazeta*, wrote an article in reply to numerous letters from readers (none of which were published in the journal) that criticized the regime's conduct of the Ginzburg-Galanskov trial. (Ginzburg and Galanskov had been tried and convicted in January. Ginzburg received five years in the labor camps; Galanskov got seven years. Galanskov subsequently died there.) In the course of his reply, which has become a notorious example of official baiting, Chakovsky gave his own suggestion for the defendants' fate: "Instead of giving such people food and drink at the nation's expense in prisons and corrective labor colonies, the responsibility for their keep should be shifted on to the American, English, or West German taxpayers."

On the day Chakovsky's article appeared, Marchenko prepared a reply. Citing the work prisoners do and the meager rations they receive, Marchenko berated Chakovsky for deliberately obscuring the truth:

In your article you assume the pose of a man with a civic conscience, as though you were genuinely concerned about our country's fate and prestige. A man in such a public position cannot justify himself by saying that he was unaware of something or ill-informed. If, indeed, you did not know until now, then you could have, and that means you should have known exactly how convicts in corrective labor colonies are fed, and at whose expense.

Marchenko concluded:

Maybe the lofty civic pathos of your article can be explained precisely by the fact that you get a bit more for it than just a bowl of gruel and a ration of black bread.

Several weeks later, on April 17, Marchenko wrote another letter on the camps, this time to the Chairman of the Red Cross Society, the Minister of Health, and other government and cultural figures. Expressing his frustration over his inability to "make my book known to the public," he explained that they "through their social position are among those most responsible for the state of society and its level of humanity and legality." He then detailed conditions in the camps, appealing to these gentlemen to demand a public investigation into the plight of political prisoners. "It is our civic duty," he reminded them, "the duty of our human conscience, to put a stop to crimes against humanity. For crime begins not with the smoking chimneys of crematoria, nor with the steamers packed with prisoners bound for Magadan. Crime begins with civic indifference."

Marchenko received only one reply to this letter. On April 29, the Deputy Chairman of the Union of Red Cross and Red Crescent Societies answered:

The committee . . . considers it necessary to point out briefly that our legislation and our Soviet conception of law look upon people who have attacked the conquests of the October Revolution as having committed a most serious offence against their people and as deserving severe punishment rather than any kind of indulgence or forbearance.

In the light of the foregoing the entirely groundless nature of all of your other assertions becomes obvious.

While Marchenko became increasingly involved with the defense of political prisoners, other events in the spring of 1968 also absorbed his attention. In Czechoslovakia, a group of liberal Communists was attempting to establish "socialism with a human face." And in the Soviet Union, several Moscow dissidents established the *Chronicle of Current Events*, an unofficial and uncensored journal designed to carry news of human rights violations. (The dissidents discourage use of the phrase "underground press" to refer to their publications for it suggests something illegal. No provision of Soviet law directly prohibits this material. Still, dissidents are discreet about their writings.)

Marchenko, along with other dissidents, followed events in Czechoslovakia as best as he could. But the Soviet press distorted the significance of the Prague Spring, alluding to "internal forces of reaction" and an "imperialist intrigue." Marchenko understood the warnings. On July 22, he wrote a letter to several newspapers in Prague and to Communist journals in Western Europe. As in *My Testimony* and his previous letters, he revealed an acute understanding of his government's behavior. He did not believe Alexander Dubcek's experiment would be allowed to continue, especially because the Czech liberals seemed determined to expose the crimes of their own country's Stalinists. Marchenko concluded:

It is understandable why our leaders hasten to intercede for the likes of Urvalek and Novotny: the precedent of making party and government leaders personally responsible before the people is a dangerous and contagious one. What if our own leaders should suddenly be required to account for deeds that have shamefully been termed "errors" and "excesses" or, even more weakly and obscurely, "difficulties experienced in the heroic past" (when it was a matter of millions of people being unjustly condemned and murdered, of torture in the KGB's dungeons, of entire peoples being declared enemies, of the collapse of the nation's agriculture, and similar trivia)?

For the KGB, this was the last straw.

On July 28, Marchenko was arrested on the street and taken to Butyrka prison, charged with infringement of identity card regulations. His friends tried to help him. Appeals were circulated, petitions drawn up. One woman, Irina Belogorodskaya, was arrested on August 8 for spreading information which "defames the Soviet social system." She had been gathering signatures in defense of Marchenko. (Later she was sentenced to a year in a labor camp.)

On August 21, 1968, the same day Warsaw Pact troops invaded Czechoslovakia, Marchenko was tried and convicted for violating internal passport regulations. The trial held no surprises except one—all of Marchenko's friends were permitted to enter the court. Probably the authorities were afraid that if his friends were not admitted but forced to stand outside the courthouse, they would become exceedingly outraged, since the trial coincided with the invasion of Prague. So about seventy of Marchenko's supporters witnessed his one-day trial. At one point, according to the *Chronicle of Current Events*, the Judge's two assistants were given the following instructions: "They were told they were dealing with a criminal so cunning and insidious that he had not broken the law, and this article of the Criminal Code was the only way of getting him into jail."

Marchenko was still a sick man. In the camps of Mordovia he had contracted meningitis, which led to the recurring infection in his middle ear. After he arrived in Moscow he had a trephining operation on his skull. He also suffered from severe internal bleeding in the stomach, and a dangerous loss of hemoglobin. Only a series of blood transfusions saved him. The court had access to his medical reports. Nonetheless, the judge sentenced him to a year in the camps, the maximum penalty for the crime he allegedly committed.

His friends had little chance to react. Four days later, seven people, among them Larisa Bogoraz and Pavel Litvinov, staged a demonstration in Red Square against the invasion of Czechoslovakia. Six of them were immediately arrested. (The seventh, a mother of two small children, was sent home.) They were tried and convicted in October. Litvinov received five years of internal exile near the Chinese border; Bogoraz—four. By December, Larisa Bogoraz reached Chuna, her place of exile, a small town in Siberia, nearly four thousand kilometers from Moscow.

During Marchenko's first year at a labor camp in Perm, *My Testimony* was published in the West. This further infuriated the authorities. While he was still serving his sentence, they were planning to convict him again.

Issue number ten of the *Chronicle*—in October 1969—gives details of Marchenko's trial in the camp. Although the report is long, it is worth being quoted in full in order to appreciate the incompentency of the regime and the precise, factual approach of the *Chronicle of Current Events.*

The *Chronicle* has already reported that Anatoly Marchenko has been sentenced again, to two years' imprisonment in strict-regime camps, under article 190-1 of the Russian Criminal Code. Marchenko's trial was held on August 22nd in the reading room of the camp zone at Nyrob, a settlement in Perm Region, and was formally considered open, although of course no one except prisoners and administrative personnel is ever allowed into the zone.

Anatoly Marchenko was charged with uttering these statements: "the Soviet Union is violating the sovereignty of other countries, and Soviet troops were sent into Czechoslovakia to suppress freedom with tanks"; "there is no democracy in the USSR, freedom of expression, of the press, of creativity does not exist"; "it is the Soviet Union who is to blame" for the events on the Sino-Soviet border. Apart from these statements, Marchenko was charged with refusing to report for work, and with declaring while in the punishment cell: "The communists have drunk all my blood." This charge was based on the testimony of two observers, i.e. punishment-cell warders, Lopanitsyn and Sobinin. Since they contradicted each other in their evidence as to the date on which Marchenko had uttered this statement, it was stated in the indictment, and later in the sentence, that he had uttered it twice—on May 14th and 15th. After the overseers had reported, KGB security officer Antonov, to whom the overseers are subordinate in their job, began to collect further material on Marchenko, and on May 31st he instituted criminal proceedings.

The charge was corroborated at the pre-trial investigation by duty warders Sedov and Dmitriyenko, as well as by the overseers' testimonies. Sedov was not summoned to appear at the trial, but his testimony was read out, in violation of the law, and also incorporated in the verdict. Dmitriyenko declared at the trial that he had not known Marchenko before, and had "decided" that the statement attributed to him in the charge had been uttered by him, but now that he had seen Marchenko at the trial and heard his voice, he was firmly convinced that Marchenko had not spoken these words. Moreover, Dmitriyenko declared that he knew who had spoken the words; and he could name the man and summon him to court. The court did not react to this declaration, and ignored Dmitriyenko's testimony in the verdict, although a court is obliged by law to explain why it had rejected any testimony which contradicts the conclusions reached in the verdict. Fellow-prisoners of Marchenko in the punishment cell, summoned to court at his request, stated that they had not heard the sentence he was charged with uttering.
    Concerning the other statements he was charged with, Marchenko said that he had held conversations with prisoners on these subjects, but that his statements had been distorted beyond recognition in the witnesses' testimony. Marchenko said he had been annoyed by the words of witness Burtsev to the effect that "Czechoslovakia ought to be crushed once and for all," since he considered the idea of crushing a man, a nation or a people to reveal hatred of mankind. During conversations about freedom of expression, the press and creativity, Marchenko had in fact replied to prisoners that no ideal freedom of expression,

press or creativity existed anywhere, nor did pure democracy, including the Soviet Union: every country had its limitations.

The prosecution witnesses recounted Marchenko's views in a primitive and arbitrary form; not one of them reproduced them accurately, and their testimony was contradictory. According to Marchenko, the case against him was a fabrication of Antonov, the camp KGB officer, who had pressurized the witnesses—all dependent on him —into giving suitable testimony. The court declared that "there was no reason not to believe the witnesses questioned at the trial, all the more so since many of them had given explanations even before proceedings began—some in their own handwriting—which confirmed the facts brought to light in court and which had led to criminal proceedings being instituted." It was precisely these "explanations," on the basis of which criminal proceedings had been instituted, which were given at interrogations conducted by the KGB chief Antonov.

The court's second argument, which it considered proof of the reliability of the witnesses' testimony, was the fact that the investigation had been headed by the Deputy-Procurator of the Perm Region and "the court has no reason to doubt his objectivity."

The composition of the court was as follows: Khrenovsky, Chairman; Rzhevin and Biryukova, People's Assessors; Baiborodina, Procurator. Marchenko conducted his own defence.

On September 30th the Russian Supreme Court considered Marchenko's appeal, and an additional appeal by the lawyer Monaknov, who spoke at the hearing. The composition of the court was: Ostroukhova, Chairman; Lukanov and Timofeyev, Members of the Court; Sorokina, Procurator. The verdict of the Perm Regional Court was upheld.

Marchenko has never elaborated on these years he spent in the camps, at least not in any writings that have reached the West. However, issue number sixteen of the *Chronicle* reported on his initial months in a new camp in the Perm district.

In spite of the medical certificates attached to Marchenko's case about the grave state of his health, and of his assignment to light work, in February and March in a temperature of 45-50 degrees centigrade of frost he was made to live in a tent and detailed to work on the unloading of firewood for trains. He was subsequently transferred to construction work—digging foundations on the territory of the camp. As a result of this Marchenko (suffering from deafness and headaches caused by meningitis, which he had contracted in previous camps) developed a hypertonic disease.

By decision of the camp administration Marchenko has been deprived of visits from his mother. His defence counsel, who had travelled to the camp to draw up a complaint for review (by the Supreme Court), was refused a meeting with his client.

Marchenko is not being given letters from his family and friends. Parcels of books (the works of Plekhanov and Pisarev, works on the history of the USSR), despatched by "Books by Post," were returned to the shop. Marchenko has been deprived of pen, paper, and a physics textbook "as having no political-educational significance"—so it is stated in the "deed of confiscation."

Marchenko was not expected to survive this term in the camps. Even Dutton, his American publishers, had little hope. On the back cover of a copy of *My Testimony*—printed in 1971—we are told that "the author is reported to be still a prisoner, but it is thought unlikely that he will be heard from again." Marchenko, however, proved them wrong.

A short time before his release, the authorities required him to choose his next place of residence, where, they told him, he would live for a year under administrative supervision. Marchenko knew he would never be allowed to live in Moscow. He submitted the names of three cities, including Chuna, where Larisa Bogoraz had several months remaining to her own term of exile. Knowing she would stay with him if he joined her there, the KGB gave Marchenko permission to live in Chuna. He went there in August 1971. He and Larisa Bogoraz were married later that year.

This was the happiest period of Marchenko's life. In September 1972, he and his wife moved to Tarusa, a city barely a hundred kilometers from Moscow. They found an old dilapidated house that Marchenko, with the skills he had learned as a young man, completely rebuilt. That winter, also, their son Pavel was born.

In Tarusa, Marchenko worked as a furnace stoker in a factory. His health, however, was precarious. During his time in camps he seemed to feel better. At home he was frequently ill; he still endured suppurating infections from his ear. Marchenko tried to find easier work. He took driving lessons, thinking he could become a truck driver. Nothing came of the idea because of his deafness. But these problems, like health and work, were normal, human difficulties; they could be tolerated.

Although Marchenko could not live in Moscow, he and his wife maintained contact with dissidents in the capital. The democratic movement, however, had changed from the time they had last lived in Moscow, five years before. The movement had achieved considerable success. Two leading dissidents—Alexander Solzhenitsyn and Andrei Sakharov—had become world figures. (Solzhenitsyn had won the Nobel Prize for Literature in 1970. Sakharov would win the Nobel Prize for Peace five years later.) And nationality groups, most notably the Crimean Tatars and Soviet Jews—with much help from Soviet liberals—managed to wring concessions from the regime. During World War II, the Tatars had been forcibly removed from their homeland in the Crimea and taken to Central Asia. The entire people had been accused of collaborating with the Nazis. By 1967, however, after many protests and appeals, they were cleared of the charge of treason, although the regime refused to permit their return to the Crimea. Soviet Jews had greater success, in part because they elicited world attention to their problems. In response, the regime was allowing thousands of Jews to leave for Israel. Finally, and perhaps most importantly, the democratic movement had transformed the moral climate among large sections of the intelligentsia.

The authorities were not left helpless. With the onset of detente, in 1972, the dissidents suffered increased repression. Although twenty-seven issues of the *Chronicle of Current*

Events had appeared regularly in Moscow for four years, the KGB managed to prevent its appearance from October 1972 until May 1974. More ominously, according to Andrei Sakharov, the regime warned that for every new appearance of the *Chronicle* "appropriate persons would be arrested and those already under arrest would be sentenced to long terms."

The crackdown on dissent was highlighted by the trial and public confessions of Pyotr Yakir and Viktor Krasin in September 1973. Innumerable others, like Bukovsky, Plyusch, Gluzman, Chornovil, and Superfin were shipped to labor camps, prisons, or the confines of mental hospitals. Other dissident and cultural figures were allowed (or virtually compelled) to emigrate. As a result, the loose coalition of nonconformists that had composed the early stages of the democratic movement had deteriorated.

The KGB had not forgotten Marchenko either. Anxious that he might be writing a new book, they often searched his house and harassed him at work. Alexander Ginzburg was also living in Tarusa at this time and the KGB, faced with Ginzburg, Marchenko, and Larisa Bogoraz in the same city, opened a special branch.

Marchenko and his wife were affected by this new pressure from the regime. They, too, began considering emigration, especially for the sake of their son. They talked of moving to Canada, living on a farm, working with their hands. In the camps Marchenko became interested in economics. Now he thought about completing his education. He was also starting to write fictional accounts of labor camp life.

But as repression continued Marchenko felt compelled to resume the struggle. On August 23, 1973, he wrote United Nations General Secretary Kurt Waldheim to inform him that the writer Andrei Amalrik might not survive his new prison term. In his letter Marchenko recalled the death of Yury Galanskov and noted that during Amalrik's previous term he had contracted meningitis and had been declared an invalid. That same month he also wrote to Willy Brandt concerning the dangers of East-West detente.

The KGB responded to this activity. On November 3, KGB agents searched his house "in connection with Case 24," the case involving the *Chronicle*. Marchenko, though, understood this was merely a pretext for examining his papers. The agents, in fact, confiscated everything written on a typewriter or by hand, although they found nothing relating to the *Chronicle*. Marchenko wrote the Procurator General, demanding his papers. Instead, on New Year's Day he received a summons to appear for interrogation by the KGB. Two agents questioned him. The first, Kharitonov, asked about his notes, warning Marchenko that they contained anti-Soviet material. Marchenko refused to cooperate. He himself could not say how they would be used. Now, however, nothing would come of them; they were not to be returned. The second agent, Major Zhernov, chose an altogether different approach. Marchenko has reproduced the gist of their remarkable discussion:

Zhernov: "You have been tried more than once, but you have not reformed and continue to engage in anti-social activity. In conformity with the Decree of the Presidium of the USSR Supreme Soviet dated December 25, 1972, I am giving you warning."
I: "What Decree is that?"

Zhernov showed me a document. So far as I understood it, the Decree stated the following: organs of police inquiry may warn persons who have committed anti-social acts not entailing criminal liability that if they continue to commit such acts, they will be held criminally liable. I was completely unable to understand the logic of the decree, and therefore asked whether it had been published anywhere—for example, in the *Vedomosti of the Supreme Soviet* (the official bulletin) or in the newspapers.

"No, Zhernov answered, "it has not been published. We are informing you about it. It exists, and has juridical force."
I: "So it's a *samizdat* document!"

Zhernov was furious: "Who are you raising your hand against? What kind of Soviet man are you?"

I: "A Soviet man should live according to written laws. But this document was slipped to you and me on the sly."

They continued:

Incidentally, during the argument with Zhernov, when I tried to show that however you looked at it the acts attributed to me did not come under the Decree, he said: "They (the acts) are not criminally punishable now, since you were already punished for them in 1968, and you can't be tried twice for the same act."
I: "So you are confirming that I was convicted for *My Testimony* and the letters? But I was tried under Article 198 for violating passport regulations..."
Zhernov: "Yes, but surely you understand that essentially it was for your activity."

Marchenko was not intimidated. A month later, in February, Alexander Solzhenitsyn was arrested and expelled from the Soviet Union. In response, a group of dissidents, including Marchenko, circulated the Moscow Appeal in his support. Soon after the KGB found a pretext to harass Marchenko further.

On April 10, Marchenko was released from his work for a short time, between the winter and summer seasons. With more free time, he worked on his house rather than simply take a vacation. The KGB, however, saw their opportunity. On May 24, he was placed under administrative supervision. Under terms set by the Tarusa police, he was required to be at home from eight in the evening to six in the morning. In addition, he was forbidden to go to bars, restaurants, or the cinema. If he wished to leave Tarusa, he first would need the permission of the police. And finally, he would have to report to the police every Monday at six p.m.

Marchenko barely tolerated such interference in his life. But out of concern for his family he tried to fulfill the provisions set by the authorities. At the same time, he continued his nonconformist activity. In July, Andrei Sakharov announced a hunger strike in support of Soviet political prisoners. Marchenko responded to his appeal, declaring a hunger strike of his own; he fasted for five days. Then, in August, the supervision became more severe. Several times Marchenko asked for permission to visit Moscow, once to bring his son to a doctor, another time to meet his mother at the train station. His requests were denied. A doctor examined Marchenko during this time, just before her own departure for the United States. She found him very weak; one ear was infected with pus.

Nonetheless, as pressure from the KGB increased, Marchenko became more obstinate. On October 11, after being refused permission to bring his sick son back to Tarusa from Moscow, he declared that he considered himself free of the supervision. In November and again in December, he was fined by the courts for violating terms of the supervision. He knew the risks he faced. By law, "malicious violation" of administrative supervision constitutes a crime, punishable by up to two years in a labor camp. Still, he did not relent. On December 10, in a letter to Nikolai Podgorny, Marchenko renounced his Soviet citizenship and declared his intention to go to the United States. At the end of December he was called to the Visa Office and encouraged to accept a visa for Israel. "If you insist on going to the U.S.," they warned him, "you'll end up being convicted for violation of supervision."

By demanding that dissidents apply for visas to Israel, the authorities seek to humiliate them and discredit both the Zionist and the democratic movements. The regime and the dissidents understand that once Soviet emigrants reach Vienna or Rome, they can arrange to stay in Europe or travel to America, regardless of the destination indicated by their exit visas. But the regime has its own motives for insisting on Israel. For years, it has tried to discredit the democratic movement by identifying its non-Jewish supporters as Jews in disguise. Even Solzhenitsyn has been dubbed "Solzhenitsker" in some of the party's propaganda. In addition, the regime is anxious to use the issue of emigration to Israel as a means of increasing the resentment of Ukrainians, Russians, and other nationalities against Jews and dissidents alike. Many Ukrainians, after all, would like to emigrate or at least visit relatives in the West, but only Jews and some dissidents appear to have this privilege.

As a matter of principle, Marchenko refused to cooperate. Again in February, he was encouraged to submit documents for his emigration. And, once more in the Visa Office, he stood by his right to emigrate to the United States. Marchenko had received invitations to come to the United States from Albert Shanker, the President of the American Federation of Teachers; PEN International, the organization of writers, had invited him to New York, as did Edward Kline, a prominent businessman involved in human rights affairs. Nonetheless, the regime proceeded against him. On the next day, February 26, his house in Tarusa was searched. The police seized rough drafts and other notes, together with manuscripts belonging to his wife. In violation of legal procedures, they refused to leave a protocol of the search. That night, Marchenko was arrested and taken to Kaluga Investigation Prison. At the time of his arrest, he declared an indefinite hunger strike and refused to cooperate with the investigation of his case.

Marchenko's behavior during this period—his appeals to the West, his refusals to accept a visa to Israel—reflect more than his obstinacy. Since the publication of *My Testimony*, he knew that his case was known in the West. His letters, also, addressed to Western statesmen or Soviet leaders, were often broadcast in Russian over stations like the BBC or Radio Liberty. In his isolation, however, without genuine access to information, he could not properly judge how closely his activities were followed in the West. The radio condenses information coming from the Soviet Union, making it seem as if the Western public actually knows and cares about internal repression. The regime, in turn, reinforces this impression by making it difficult for dissenters to maintain contact with the West. Ironically, both the regime and its critics share an identical illusion, for the West, in general, is not thirsting for news from the Soviet Union. Marchenko made a tragic miscalculation. He believed that his appeals, his renunciation of Soviet citizenship, his insistence on emigrating to America, would compel the regime to relent. But he overestimated Western interest in internal Soviet developments.

A decade ago, at the outset of the democratic movement, the Western press exaggerated the influence of this small group of people, oversold them, as it were, as if several thousand people could reverse the drift of Russian history. In recent years newspapers have not paid consistent attention to dissident activity in the Soviet Union. Now, when an equal number of appeals still circulates, when dissenters are still removed to prisons and mental hospitals, the press seems less anxious to cover the ongoing repression.

Furthermore, Marchenko's character increased his willingness to challenge the regime. After years of opposition and suffering he had come to believe firmly in the need to place himself in danger, as if only the reprisals he faced could confirm the legitimacy and justice of his behavior. One incident, in particular, illustrates his readiness to suffer. In 1972, after Marchenko had rejoined Larisa Bogoraz in Chuna, they traveled to a small village near the Manchurian border to visit Pavel Litvinov. One evening together they listened to a Russian broadcast of the Voice of Israel: an Israeli professor discussing the difference between Judasim and Christianity, specifically over the issue of martyrdom. Listening to the program, Litvinov and his wife, Maya, agreed with the Jewish point of view, that life has the highest priority and that martyrdom should be avoided, except under the most compelling circumstances. Marchenko, however, took the Christian position, believing in the need to seek martyrdom, regardless of the consequences. Few of his fellow dissenters would accept this attitude.

Marchenko's stubbornness, his allegiance to truth and opposition to injustice make him a genuine Russian hero: but not, necessarily, a simple or particularly likable one. Other dissidents, too, oppose the regime, run needless risks, suffer arbitrary punishments. At the same time, most of them, most notably those who are intellectuals, reserve a part of their energy and some of their time for personal or professional pursuits. They resist becoming full-time revolutionaries and hesitate to relinquish their creative ambitions and personal loyalties.

From the time of his arrival in Moscow in 1966, Marchenko transformed his life into a virtual crusade on behalf of Soviet political prisoners. As his involvement deepened, so, too, did his anger and intolerance. Friends who knew him in Moscow remember how his opinions hardened, how he came to view issues in starker, more simple terms. His life became synonymous with his cause. He grew impatient with those who hesitated to sign an appeal. The restraints others experienced, like the potential loss of employment, or the responsibility to one's family, did not move him. Even his love for his infant son did not deter him from refusing a visa to Israel. Principle alone dictated his behavior.

In part, Marchenko's attitude reflects his origins and the vicissitudes of his life. In contrast to virtually all of his fellow dissidents, he never completed his formal education. Since 1958, except for occasional periods, he has lived in labor camps, prison, or exile. Yet he also came to regard himself as a writer and a spokesman. The authorities ironically resented his social and intellectual pretensions. For the police, themselves members of the lower classes, Marchenko's familiarity with Jews and intellectuals was offensive; they knew how to remind him of his proper place. Marchenko, in turn, never learned to mitigate reprisals by the regime. His own defiance invited the harsh treatment that other dissidents learned to avoid.

Marchenko was prepared for prison. He kept mittens, warm socks, a toothbrush, and soap near the door. His wife had agreed to go to Moscow if he were arrested in order to be with family and friends. In jail he refused to answer questions, give fingerprints, sign documents. The warders beat him—with keys, their boots and their fists. The investigation itself was perfunctory; the officer in charge did not even know what material had been confiscated. Still, Marchenko waited five weeks for his trial to begin.

The whole time he continued his hunger strike. After eight days without food, he was dragged from his cell to be force fed. He refused to walk by himself, to sit down, to open his mouth. They manacled his hands behind his back so tightly that his shoulders ached for weeks. When he resisted the spreader, they fed him through his nostrils. When the doctors came to inject glucose, he distorted his skin and muscles in order to impede the needle.

Marchenko's *From Tarusa to Siberia* (1976) is now appearing for the first time in English. Written in Siberian exile, it is a short memoir of his hunger strike and trial. "My protest was a reaction to coercion, and the more brutal that coercion became, the more extreme became the form of my protest." His own conduct surprised, even repelled him. "Do I sit down on the stool voluntarily or allow strange hands to pin me down?". . . "Each time the entire scene provoked in me an idiotic feeling. I could not define for myself at what point my refusal to submit voluntarily stopped being a protest and became simply asinine stubbornness." Once before he had attempted a hunger strike—in 1961, after his conviction for treason. He was force fed and next day gave in. This time he was more determined.

The trial took place in Kaluga on the thirty-third day of his hunger strike. The courtroom was open. Twenty of Marchenko's friends and relatives, including Andrei Sakharov, attended. Marchenko was led in by several guards. He looked bad. His wrists were handcuffed behind his back. At the defendant's bench he almost collapsed; the guards held him up. He told the court that his copy of the indictment had been taken from him on the way to the courthouse, in violation of judicial procedure. In fact, he had not been informed that his trial was about to begin. The court disregarded this. Then Marchenko asked that his wife be allowed to defend him. The court denied his request, appointing a lawyer whom Marchenko had never seen. In response to these abuses, Marchenko refused to take part in the proceedings, reserving only his right to a final plea.

The trial then continued over the predicted charge— violation of administrative supervision. Several policemen were called. No one cross-examined them. During a recess, his wife and friends, claiming that they could refute the accusations, asked the defense lawyer to call them as witnesses. At first, he refused. Later, though, he asked the court to allow them to testify. But the judge refused, claiming that they had been in the courtroom during the testimony of other witnesses.

Marchenko presented no defense; he spoke only to make his final plea.

. . . Neither the investigator nor the court has shown any interest in the fact that until October 11 I complied with the conditions of the supervision, and that I ceased to comply with them only when I was finally convinced of their humiliating character. After the summer, all my requests prompted by a concern for my family had been denied. I asked for permission to meet my mother—who is not only aged but illiterate— at the station in Moscow. I was refused. To visit my sick child in Moscow: refused. To see my aged mother off: refused. When my son got sick, it was thought he might have scarlet fever, I asked permission to take him to Moscow, since there was no pediatrician in Tarusa. For four days, Volodin, the police chief, gave me the run-around: "Come back tomorrow; come back after lunch." Finally, on the fourth day, he told me bluntly that he had not received an answer. Who, I wonder, was supposed to answer that kind of request? After all, the law states that supervision is carried out by the regular police. I went back once more.

The deputy chief told me my request had been denied. Then I told him I would refuse to comply with the supervision, and took my wife and sick child to Moscow. After that outrageous incident I considered myself free from supervision. I issued a statement saying that I had been outlawed in my own country. I addressed that statement to the world public. It is hard enough for one person to oppose a gang of bandits, but it is even harder to defend oneself against gangsters calling themselves the state. I do not repent of what I did. I love freedom. But if I am living in a state where concern for one's family and relatives, or love for and devotion to one's child, are criminal, I prefer a prison cell. Where else would I be tried for such acts? I was put in a situation where I had to choose: to renounce my family, or to become a criminal.

Marchenko was convicted. Surprisingly, the court sentenced him to four years of exile in Chuna, a punishment not included in the Code for violation of administrative supervision. His wife and child could join him. His fellow prisoners in Kaluga were amazed; hunger strikes are not supposed to count. "You're going to be free," they told him.

Another twelve days passed before he began his journey to Chuna. The officers on the train did not know of his hunger strike. He had to tell them himself, refusing his rations. His dossier contained no word of his hunger strike, although across the front was printed in bold type: INCLINED TO SUICIDE. He was not held separately, no doctor accompanied him—conditions required for hunger strikers. They refused to recognize his condition, so he was not force fed. In crowded trains, at switching-points, in halls full of convicts, Marchenko was treated like the other prisoners, forced to drag his mattress, to stand long hours. He was in the eighth week of his hunger strike. His last reserves of strength abated. After eight days in transit, he could no longer move. In the corridor, a warder argued with his boss, refusing to answer for a prisoner's impending death. Marchenko realized it was time to relent. He broke his strike the next morning, chewing slowly on a spoonful of gruel.

His deportation lasted another month. Arriving in

Chuna, Marchenko issued a statement through his friends in Moscow. He thanked all those who spoke out in his defense.

After all he has endured, Anatoly Marchenko has not relinquished his dignity or his determination. Living in Siberian exile, he managed to write *From Tarusa to Siberia*. In 1975, he suffered an attack of neuritis and was rushed to a hospital in Irkutsk. Although he recovered, the authorities forced him to leave the hospital well before he regained his strength. Marchenko persists. In the spring of 1976 he joined a small group of activists that seeks to monitor Soviet compliance with the Helsinki accords.

Marchenko's term of exile ended in September 1978, but not before the authorities tried to detain him again. In July, a local investigator asked two former criminals living in Chuna to plant a small bag of gold in Marchenko's house. They refused and one of the men then warned Marchenko of the plot. The investigator had assured them that someone would be found to cooperate. Word of this new threat reached Moscow and was passed to the West. Articles and protests immediately appeared. The authorities backed down. In September, Marchenko was allowed to leave Chuna. With his family he traveled to the Caucasus to visit his mother and to rest. Later that fall, they reached a place not far from Moscow where they are living today.

A century ago a Russian nobleman named Peter Chaadaev published a "Philosophical Letter" critical of Russian culture and society. The government ordered confiscation of the journal in which the letter had appeared. The editor was sent to Siberia, the censor dismissed, and the daily press forbidden to mention the author's name. Anticipating his latter-day successors, the Emperor Nicholas I proclaimed Chaadaev officially insane. He was ordered to remain at home, and, for a time, forced to endure the periodic visits of a doctor. Naturally, the essay became the valued possession of every Russian intellectual. Book dealers sold clandestine copies while hundreds of manuscripts passed from hand to hand in the salons of Moscow and Petersburg.

Chaadaev's notoriety, the details of his treatment by the Emperor, only confirmed the pessimism and shame his essay expressed over the backward condition of Russian life. "One of the most deplorable things in our unique civilization," he wrote, "is that we are still just beginning to discover truths which are trite elsewhere. . . . What has long since constituted the very basis of social life in other lands is still only theory and speculation for us."

Today, Anatoly Marchenko and his fellow dissidents face an even harsher silence than that which restrained Chaadaev. Marchenko writes in *My Testimony*, "Clean and honest actions are not done in the dark." Yet in a land of silence, the truth, too, provides its own isolation. Once a nurse from the camp hospital left for a holiday. She did not reveal to the friends she met that she worked in a labor camp. But, as she later told the prisoners, she happened to mention incidents from her work, that one patient had a spoon in his stomach, another had swallowed nails, or chessmen, or glass. Her friends at the resort decided that she was abnormal and avoided her company. "She told us this on one of the evenings when we gathered in the treatment room. And all of a sudden," Marchenko remembers, "we seemed to see properly for the first time everything that surrounded us, the whole savagery and fantastic incredibility of the situation we were in, of these ordinary stories of ours, and of this hospital behind barbed wire under the armed guard of tommy gunners in their watch towers."

Pasha and Anatoly Marchenko, 1974

FROM TARUSA TO SIBERIA

Pasha with Larisa, 1974

Author's Foreword

When I was discharged from prison camp in 1966, I considered it my civic duty to write down and make public what I had seen. This I did in my book *My Testimony*.

Then I decided to try my hand at creative writing. While I was interned in the Perm region, from 1968 to 1971, I conceived and planned a tale entitled *Live as Others Live (Zhivi kak vse)*, having nothing at all to do with prison camps. The subject was a nonconformist and his tragic fate. I am quite unable to measure the success or failure of the effort, as my rough drafts and notes for the story were systematically confiscated by the Great Archivist—the KGB—in the course of their overt and covert searches of my belongings in the camp and at home. In order to insure the safety of a draft which eluded the searchers, I have not yet risked showing it to anyone. And so the only expert opinion I can quote is the following comment by KGB officials: " . . . these notes constitute material in draft which could be used for writing anti-Soviet works."

In putting pen to paper I do not aim to write anything "anti-Soviet" or "Soviet." I write my own way. What interests me is my conception and the fate of my hero.

In the meantime, my own destiny continued to reveal its design, and I had to postpone further work on my story. Somewhere I read this precept: if you have witnessed a natural disaster, a foreign invasion, a subjugation or the like, write down everything you have seen yourself or heard from others; it is your duty to do so. Duty once more compels me to tell what I think has not yet been told by anyone and what I went through myself. *From Tarusa to Siberia* is my story.

□□□□□

The story is a sketch and not notes from a journal. I wrote it in exile, from memory, so that a few things have probably been left out. I intentionally omitted certain marginal episodes, which I may return to one day. The full meaning of many events became clear to me only much later.

□□□□□

February 25, 1975. I was undergoing the customary search at the militia station. I had nothing on me worth confiscating: already in December I had picked out an old pair of pants to wear in jail, and I was wearing them now along with a warm sweater and a quilted jacket. Since December my shopping bag had hung on the hook at home, ready to go, with some underwear, warm socks and mittens, soap, toothbrush and toothpaste—and that was it. I would not need any food. They just took away my empty shopping bag and gave me a receipt for it. Everything else went with me to the prison cell.

But first they started to make out the report. I stated my name and refused to answer any further questions. And I refused to let my fingerprints be taken or to sign some kind of official document. I had decided ahead of time not to take part in any of their formal procedures: if I was going to be treated in an arbitrary and violent manner, at least it would be without my cooperation.

One officer at the search favored firm action. "One way or another, willing or not, we'll get his fingerprints. Put the cuffs on him and let's go!"

The militia men on duty showed indignation and amazement: "Why take it out on us? We only work here."

How often had I heard those words, and how many times would I hear them again!

Into the duty room walked another person who "only

works here"—Kuzikov, the parole officer assigned to keep an eye on me. He did not give the orders, so why blame him? But the order was given; he wrote a false report on me; and in court he would bear false witness. Maybe for that he would earn official thanks, while I would be sent to prison camp. Kuzikov stopped a few steps away from me and demonstratively drew a small pistol from his pocket. I turned away and did not see what he did with the pistol; I only heard a click close to my ear. What a fool! His finger was bleeding: the hero was wounded in action when he dragged a woman into the station against her will. The woman, who had been visiting my wife and me, was brought in and I only got a glimpse of her; we scarcely had time to exchange nods. This was probably my last encounter as a free man.

In the cell I was alone, thank Heaven. The scene was so familiar to me that I felt as if I had never been away from prison. I threw my jacket onto the bed—a cot consisting of wooden planks. "I lay me down on one of my wings and covered myself with the other."

But I had a hard time falling asleep. There is nothing worse than thinking of home when you are in jail, but it is impossible not to do so. At the time of my previous incarcerations it was easier, for I had no family. But now no sooner did I close my eyes than I saw the picture: Pashka would wake up early in the morning, stand up on his legs and shake his crib. He would laugh and call to me: at night and in the morning he acknowledged only me; his mother slept in the other room. On the evening of the search it was I who put him to bed and rocked him to sleep, and now I could almost feel the pressure of that little head against my shoulder. I wondered how my wife was managing to cope with the child and all the housework. We had agreed ahead of time that she should leave Tarusa immediately and go to Moscow, where friends and relatives would help her, but she would still have a difficult time of it.

And I wondered what the next day would bring in my

own life. Obviously they would not leave me in Tarusa, and the trial could be held at any time, as there was nothing to investigate: the papers were all made out in advance—violation number one, violation number two, and so on.

26 February. I was awakened in the morning by the noise of the door-lock. For some reason, all the locks in prison doors work with a terrible racket. A "Decembrist," a prisoner accompanied by the duty officer for the preliminary detention ward, set down a mug of boiling hot water and one ration of bread onto my cot.

"Breakfast," he announced.

"I will not accept food," I replied.

I did not go into any discussion with the duty officer.

Around nine o'clock they got me up again, this time to go out. In the guard room they gave me back my property: one shopping bag. That meant they were going to take me away from Tarusa. But where to? The paddy wagon of Tarusa is a minibus without compartments, its window covered with a coarse screen. There were two of us in the back—one militiaman and myself—and another man, in addition to the driver in front, who carried a briefcase. Through the window I had a good view of the little old streets of Tarusa, and I said goodbye to them. I thought: if we turn right, past the garage, that will mean we are headed for Serpukhov or possibly Moscow; if we go left and up it will mean Kaluga. We went almost past my house, but I could not see it around the corner.

The vehicle turned left. I had a strong feeling, almost a conviction, that Larisa was very close by. So I was not surprised when I actually saw her. She was walking past the milk store and pulling Pashka on a sled, coming from the direction in which we were driving. The child's red winter coat stood out a mile away: it was the only one of its kind in Tarusa. Larisa saw the paddy wagon. She stopped and looked as hard as she could. When the vehicle reached the point where she stood, I knocked at the window. Larisa waved, bent over to say something to Pashka, and then just stood there for a long time staring at the police car as it struggled up the icy street.

Well, at least now she would know that I was no longer in Tarusa. Would the three of us ever meet again? When? And where?

I knew the road well. Over the past two and a half years I had traveled it often—the most recent occasion being at the end of January when I was summoned to the *oblast* visa and registration office (OVIR) to fill out forms for leaving the country. Before that, the same people had wheedled and threatened: either you apply for an exit visa to Israel or else you will be hauled into court and sent to prison camp. And that is what happened.

We passed through Petrishchevo, the place where my wife and I miraculously succeeded in getting permission to settle after two months of fruitless effort. Then came Ferzikovo, where Ginzburg had been brought to trial[1] —likewise for violation of parole. Was I to be tried here, too? Evidently not: through the window I glimpsed the white statue of an elk on the left hand side of the road, and we drove on. Now it was clear that our destination was Kaluga.

During the ride I turned over in my mind, once again, my plan of non-participation in procedures. But why the hell try? All of us—I myself, and the people on top who decided my fate, and those who set about implementing the decision —we all knew that parole was not the question, that the trial would be a put-up job, that the evidence would be faked, that I was being sent up not because of whether or not I was home, but because I was who I was. This country was not the place for me: I was a thorn in their flesh and they in mine. So why in blazes should I suddenly be meek as a lamb behind bars? Just because I would be out of sight and far away from friends? On the other hand, it was humiliating and disgusting to be fighting over trifles all the time with everyone—the parole officer, the prison officials and every other small fry. My

[47]

quarrel was not with them; I was aiming higher; but I would never see the higher-ups face to face. Finally we arrived. Now the fun would begin.

□□□□□

"Get over to that table."

"No."

"We have to have your fingerprints."

"I refuse."

"You what? Nobody is asking you, we're telling you!"

"Go ahead and make me. I won't cooperate. I will resist."

There were several people in the room where they brought me for this procedure: a prisoner co-opted as photographer, and three guards. One of these, a fat and genial-looking officer, was involved in telling some kind of long story. They were all dumbfounded by my insolence; that first sergeant piped up: "Hey, big shot, no broken bones yet? You'll start begging on your knees in a minute. We'll tie you in knots—you're asking for it. And you'll get a taste of this." And he stuck a huge iron key in front of my nose, one of a bunch he held in his hand. I was surprised to see how quickly he changed from a good-natured joker to a bloodshot fury. The veins swelled on his thick neck. Seething with hatred, trembling with a desire to lay into me, he sprang from his chair. What had I done? Had I insulted him, offended him in some way?

The others, too, waxed indignant and threatened me. Meanwhile, someone had called the duty officer. The young man appeared and they explained the situation to him.

"What's all this nonsense about?" he asked me. "No nonsense, just my way of protesting." "Protest all you want out there, but not in here. We don't give a hang about your protests. Now how about the fingerprints?"

"No."

The officer told me to turn about-face. I obeyed. Clumsily he put the handcuffs on me, my arms bent behind my back. Then he checked to see if they were tight enough. The sergeant jumped up and began to pull on them himself, cursing me all the while and hitting me in the back with his key; finally he gave another jump and struck the handcuff-chain with his knee. So he really meant it when he said he would tie me into knots. I saw red; I thought my arms would be thrown out of joint. The blow from that big hulk would have knocked me over, but the solicitous guards held me and kept me from falling. I was hit again hard in the side with fists and in the back with the key.

"Stand up straight!"

When I stopped swaying, the blows ceased.

"Follow me," said the officer. He led the way, and I followed with my hands tied behind me. Two guards—a sergeant and the fat first sergeant—walked close beside and in back of me. On the way to the stairs they did not beat me; they only cursed and threatened. But at the landing another blow of the key made me totter against the railing. The noise caused the officer to turn around. He hit me once in the ribs and again below the belt. They dragged me down the stairs and along the corridor, kicking me in the legs with their boots and pelting me with fists and keys on my back, in my ribs and stomach. In the hall we met a major, who, I later learned, was the deputy commander of the prison. The major stepped aside and let us pass.

They shoved me into a solitary cell and threw me on the cement floor where I hit my head. My jacket, hat and socks came flying in after me.

Unable to lift myself from the floor, I did not even try to change my position and just lay there, face downward. My wrists were so numb that I could not feel them any more, but there was a sharp pain in my shoulder. I was convinced that the first sergeant had dislocated my right arm. And I felt pain in my ribs: they continued to hurt for two weeks.

Now my situation became even more emotional: I had personal accounts to settle with my jailors.

The cell door opened. "Well, how about those fingerprints?"

"Forget it."

"Then just go on lying there."

This dialogue was repeated three or four times, after which, to my surprise and joy, they removed the handcuffs. But I could not get up right away. I crawled over on my jacket, lay there for awhile, and then sat up. Toward evening the reason for the guards' kindness became clear: they took me to the interrogator.

The interrogator on duty was a woman.

Sometimes God gives people names to fit their jobs. One well-known KGB interrogator is named Syshchikov.

This woman was the interrogator of the Tarusa public prosecutor's office *(prokuratura)*. She was about thirty-five or forty years old. Her tired face wore absolutely no expression and showed no interest in anything whatsoever. Her voice was dull and monotonous. It was clear that her work was simply an exhausting way to earn an income, and nothing more. She had to go to Kaluga to see her "charges," a three-hour trip each way on a rough Russian road; it was impossible to get home to her family on time. This was written all over her sad face. And those charges were not exactly angels, no doubt. I was one of the worst: I took the search warrant and did not give it back; I refused to talk or answer questions or to sign any papers. But the woman did not get angry or irritated. With weary indifference she took her notes and recited her lines: "Your attitude can only harm you. . . . You refuse to recognize our authority, but that does not change anything. . . . Marchenko! Are you listening to me?"

What can I say against that interrogator? She was calmly indifferent and did not nag; it was really easy not to listen to her mumblings, but just to sit and rest after the spell in solitary. Privately I thought perhaps I should feel sorry for this poor harassed woman. Every word she wrote for the file on me was dictated from above—probably by the KGB. She would not even answer my wife's questions about my condition without going to check first. Nor did she reject the attorney's petition on her own, and would not touch it until she got orders to do so. She knew perfectly well that the case was phony, that the statements made by Kuzikov were mendacious. She had a list of witnesses who could refute those statements, but she did not summon any of them for questioning. At the same time, she was handed a fixed witness named Trubitsyn, whose false testimony she conscientiously put into the file. Yet she did not include in her file a single piece of paper confiscated in the course of the search: she herself said that she examined none of this material, but left it all unopened and turned it over to the KGB. Maybe, after all, I was her easiest customer. In a case like mine, personal responsibility and initiative were out of place: you just do as you are told and you will not be blamed for anything. And on the other hand she would have risked little by showing some small degree of professional pride, for she was a lowly employee without greater ambitions. The rough ride to Kaluga did not wear her out as much as did the burden of trying to please her superiors.

But why should I feel sorry for her? The hands of such ciphers as she are what tore me away from my wife and son and tossed me into prison. And I would be in the clutches of others before very long.

□□□□□

I was put into a fancy cell: a three-man cell instead of a common dormitory, a real bed instead of boards, with real bedding—mattress, pillow, blanket, pillowcase and mattress pad. Peace and quiet. My two cell-mates played chess and dominoes from reveille to taps and left me alone.

Time passes quickly in prison if you can pace the floor:

it is easier to think when you walk. But the cell was small, with no room to move about. And soon it became difficult for me to move at all, as I began to have headaches. Most of the time I lay on the bed, and read when there was something to read. Too bad there was nothing to read. The library gave out one book every ten days—three books, that is, to our cell. We could not pick or choose: the librarian would stick five or six books into the feed-bin; we would keep three and she would take the rest of them away. The librarian was a genuine slut. If you asked her to leave an extra book, or to let you select, she would answer in words to this effect: "They did not send you here to read books." Or: "You try to please them all, you got no time to put your pants back on." It would be interesting to know what the top MVD³ brass would say to that—the men who dreamed up the ten-day book restriction.

The three beds in the cell were placed as follows: one opposite the door under the window; and the other two along the side walls with a narrow space between them. Facing me was a fellow from Leningrad, about 35 or 40, with the same name as I—Anatoly. He always referred to his home town in the old style as Petersburg. He was a professional criminal and pickpocket, with good grounds for calling himself an old-timer, since he was serving his eighth sentence. And there I was, thinking that pickpockets were becoming extinct. Igor, who occupied the bed below the window, was from Kaluga. He said he was an engineer, and maybe he was for all I know. He said that he had not been to prison camp, but that this would be his second trial. The first time he was arrested for hitting a militiaman (who was drunk, he said, though he was sober). They sentenced him to two years and gave him a pardon on the spot. It seems that in our country now there is a special amnesty declared every year for short-term offenders combined with compulsory labor for a prescribed period on industrial construction sites and the like. One such amnesty took place when I was interned at Perm, in

March. I was put into a cell with amnestied prisoners (referred to as "chemists," because the majority of them were assigned to construction of major chemical installations): we were shipped out together.

Now Igor was accused of stealing three hundred rubles from a female relative of his. According to him, he was innocent, but his story did not hang together. Possibly he was drunk, took the money, hid it in the pack of cigarettes where it was found, and could not remember anything. At the most he would get three years; but more likely he would be pardoned and sent to the chemical works.

My cellmates were easy to live with, and that was the main thing. What got me was something else. . . .

Each morning three bread rations were put into the feed-bin. One of these portions went back untouched, as I was on a hunger strike. My two fellow prisoners ate theirs. They ate breakfast twice—the first time each on his own bed with a bowlful of prison *kasha*, and about an hour later sitting together over their own personal food supplies, which they shared. The man from Petersburg bought his at the prison store, while his companion also had packages from home.

The cell was furnished with a single stool which stood in the space between my bed and the one opposite. Anatoly sat on his bed and Igor made himself at home on mine, near the head, while I lay there having no other place to go. On the stool, literally under my nose they spread their raw bacon, sausage, crackers, sugar and other authorized foodstuffs. They took their time eating and talked all the while. They made an even bigger show out of supper. Around five o'clock the guard came to get the tea-kettle. My two cellmates then proceeded to "set the table" for tea. And again right in front of me all the food came out; meanwhile they chatted or listened to the radio. The kettle was brought back full of boiling water about an hour or so later and the long tea party got going again. Some two hours later the regulation supper arrived—a plate of soup per person. Often my cellmates emptied the soup out into the toilet bowl, as they were not hungry. But then, with their own food, they would go through the tea ritual once more before lights out.

They did not forget that I was there. In the beginning they invited me to join them: the Petersburg oldtimer viewed the hunger strike as a futile gesture making no impression on "them" while destroying the striker. Since I refused the invitations, they stopped insisting, but they included me in the table talk. They showed not the slightest embarrassment at consuming their pork and cookies right in front of a starving man. (After my trial, when I was in another cell, my neighbor behaved quite differently, trying to do his eating while I read or slept. Obviously the situation created by the prison administration bothered him more than it did me.)

So was it harassment? Were they under orders to tease my appetite? Was it a cruel method of breaking the hunger strike? Or did neither of them give a damn? Perhaps. At any rate it is customary to isolate hunger-strikers from other prisoners, at some point if not right away. If they were trying to break my strike or merely to get my goat they did not succeed. (They doubtless had some such thing in mind. Even the prosecutor dangled the bait: "Your wife complains that you are not being kept in solitary confinement while you are on a hunger strike. Anatoly Tikhonovich, does it irritate you to see others eat?" What a thing to ask a man who has not eaten for over a month!) Neither the sight nor the smell of food, nor the sound of smacking and chewing, aroused the slightest sense of hunger in me. During the entire 54 days of my hunger strike I had no desire to eat, and my mouth never watered at the sight of the pork and cookies being consumed in front of me. To my own amazement I was never irritated by my cellmates with their endless chess games, their stupid empty conversations and their demonstrative gluttony. My reactions had been different before; but now, I thought, I am getting old and have become more tolerant. Soon after I stopped my hunger strike, however, I noticed that I was beginning to be irritated again by my fellow prisoners the way I used to be.

Only once did I envy them their fare: they each got a pickle for lunch. It was not that I was hungry or wanted to eat—I simply craved a pickle. I thought I could hear their teeth biting through the crunchy skin of the pickle, I could almost taste it in my mouth and that tantalized me no end. But my mouth did not water, as it was totally dry; my lips were parched and cracking, and I picked and chewed bits of skin from them. Invariably I drank several swallows of water in the morning, even when I wasn't thirsty.

Apparently the pickles weren't too good, for my companions only took a bit or two and threw the rest into the garbage. They often did the same thing with pieces of bread. Were they putting on an act for my benefit? Did they check the garbage in the morning to see if the bread they discarded in the evening was still there? But, believe me, I really did not feel like eating—not during the first five days, which they say are the hardest, not during the last week, not even during the very last day. All in all, I cannot say that my sensations were special or different in the earlier or later stages of the strike. The beginning and the end seemed all the same. Of course it is nonsense to call the first day a hunger strike. Everybody probably goes without food for a day or two at some point. Weakness sets in gradually and imperceptibly from day to day, so that today you feel just like yesterday and tomorrow like today. Some people can keep track of their own reactions more precisely, no doubt, and note the critical points, since different people have different sensations. For my part, I divided the strike into three stages by purely external signs: the first, eight days up until the force-feeding began; the second, 37 days during which I was fed by force; and the third, the last eight days of the strike, without any food at all, while I was being transferred.

March 4. The prison commander. The Kaluga prison I was put into was not called a prison at all, but a SIZO—investigative isolator number one *(sledstvennyi izoliator).* A harmless-sounding name, but in fact just another jail, with solitary cells, bars on the windows, and all the other typical prison features. The age of technology and design was also in evidence: the massive gates swung open at the push of a button, and the visitors' room was particularly up-to-date—with sheet-glass compartments and cabins equipped with talking apparatus. (And maybe listening devices, too? Was all that paid for in foreign currency? Or had they learned to manufacture it themselves?) It was an unforgettably powerful experience. When you heard some kind of quacking in the receiver instead of the familiar voice, you felt that you were already in the middle of the glorious future.

All of these innovations were, of course, the work of the prison commander. This was already evident in the approaches to his office where the walls, instead of wearing the usual tedious muddy-colored coat of paint, were decoratively tiled without any kind of regulation symmetry—more like a modern cafe where young people go. The office itself had a more sober aspect, with polished dark wood panelling, spacious windows, and, to the left of the desk, a control panel with blinking colored lights, telephones and microphones. The occupant was a youngish major, smoothly combed and cleanshaven, with just the right degree of stoutness, efficiency and affability. On his lapel he wore the blue diamond-shaped insignia of some higher educational institution—maybe the MVD Academy, or a law school or a university, I do not know.

The guard who brought me there vanished into thin air and only two people were left in the office: Prisoner Marchenko and the prison commander. I did not ask to see him; he had summoned me, and now I would find out why. I had every intention of sticking to my guns—answering no questions and refusing to get into a discussion. But things did not work out that way. From the outset the major took a man-to-man tone, as in a conversation where each participant defends his own point of view, and I was unable to resist. I took part in the discussion even though I was fully aware that it was pointless. My interlocutor seemed terribly serious and altogether prepared to understand me and to sympathize with me. And he expected me in return to behave with proper understanding and respect, but he did not insist. He expounded his views, from which it followed logically that I was behaving in an unreasonable and incorrect manner, and that there were other ways out of my situation. Of course it was barbaric to prevent a man from visiting his wife and child; there was no justification for that. He himself, this officer, would behave the same way if he were in my shoes. "In such a huge and multinational country as ours, it is not surprising that there are instances and violations of legality. But you will agree, Anatoly Tikhonovich, that these are the exceptions! And they are rare! And the press and control agencies are trying to do something about it."

So that is what I was supposed to do: write, and complain through every channel, and legality would triumph—of course assuming that I had stated the situation correctly. Why should I fight savagery with savagery and self-laceration?

I looked at my interlocutor. There was no sign of hypocrisy or falsehood or ulterior motive in his face. Before me sat an honest Soviet man, who firmly believed that arbitrary rule was a thing of the past in our country. He, the prison commander, could be himself—honest, decent and intelligent, and everything works in favor of his so being. His very position calls for honesty above all. "Anatoly Tikhonovich, apparently a mistake has been made in your case, but you are taking the wrong stand and only making matters worse when they could be corrected."

There is no way to prove that no error has been

committed, that this ordeal was planned and carried out accordingly, and that the law in this case was merely a screen full of holes through which you could seen hands manipulating the strings of puppets. To whom could you complain and whom would you blame?

"As you see it, Anatoly Tikhonovich, you alone are a decent person and a man of principle, and all the other 240 million are cowardly puppets. But that is not true! Take me, for instance. I honor the law above all, and our law does not contradict the highest humanitarian morality. On the contrary." And he shuffled pamphlets and instruction sheets on his desk as if to show me how conscientiously he adhered to regulations.

Although I had not intended to complain, I could not hold back: "All right, let's not discuss the laws. But here in your prison I was beaten, which presumably is against the rules. And I was not cutting up or fighting. Shouldn't refusal to obey the rules be punished in some other way? Suppose I had come in here without reporting and saluting, and you would hit me in the face. 'Rules' are posted on the wall of the cell, but they do not protect me from such artitrary treatment."

The prison commander did not shout: that'sa lie! Nor did he put on a show of indignation: how did they dare! He coolly wrote down the details of the beating—when, how and why.

"But I don't want to start any investigation or trouble. I am not complaining, I was just giving an example."

"No, no! We don't need your condescension. I will look into this today, and if the facts are confirmed, the guilty persons will be punished." (That fat first seargeant will confirm that he hit me with the keys? Besides, it's unlikely that the major we passed in the hall was surprised by what he saw.)

So why get into discussions like that? I know that, regardless of how sincere or hypocritical the official may look, whether he is tactful or uncouth, whether he goes off half-cocked or keeps his cool—it is all a lie anyway—a lie and a sham. Today he talks to me across the table, but tomorrow, if new instructions come in, he will stuff a whole cell with people like me and strangle us all with his bare hands. Some other officer would sense the way the wind is blowing and take the initiative without waiting for orders. His whole way of looking at things was not thought out on his own, but stuffed readymade into his head, turning the man into an automaton. Change the signals and he will act differently. Why bother to argue with him? It was ironic, the jailor and the jailbird talking to each other on an equal footing. During those two hours or so I was unaware of the disparity in our situations—don't tell me I was falling for that equality act!

And the major himself? He called me in on account of a hunger strike and fingerprinting, and off he went in all directions—legality, emigration, psychology. Surely he did not think that he could convert me to his views, make me see the light. I do not think he was a fool. The conversation could have been a brief one, but this busy man spent a whole two hours jabbering with me. Maybe he had no one to talk to. Indeed, what kind of friends or colleagues could he possibly have? There were so many numbskulls with whom you could drink vodka but not converse. And as for outside acquaintances, I could just hear it: "That's Lucy's husband," and in a whisper, "he is in charge of the prison." Kaluga society would hardly be overjoyed to have him around. So his social life was limited to his own bunch. And he could not very well discuss legal questions with them. Not a chance.

He probably saw me as a kind of punching-bag for training himself in argumentation and self-assertion.

But maybe my motives were the same in that bout. Larisa told me later that she detested the major at first sight, that she could smell fraud and falsehood the minute she walked in the door. Yet after that "friendly" chat I almost was ready to believe that he was a black sheep, and that my tightly-knit philosophy (of which a fundamental thesis is:

[59]

there is a pig assigned to every pigslot) was beginning to show holes. But Prisoner Marchenko and the prison commander would have occasion for exchanges on a more formal basis.

March 7. Medicine. As I was on a hunger strike I came into close contact with the medics the whole time I was at Kaluga. Prior to force-feeding they called me in several times to examine me, check my blood pressure, and temperature. In the space of 45 days they took my blood several times for analysis. I did not go on sick call on my own (except for one time shortly before the trial), but I did not refuse to be examined. I only told the doctor that I would not make any statement about my condition in connection with the hunger strike: if need be, let them find out for themselves and do as they see fit.

The doctor was a nice woman, no longer young. She was outraged: "The medical service has nothing to do with your problems. We are here to help people, so you should take your protest elsewhere."

"I don't have anything against medicine or against you personally."

"Then what's the trouble? Why do you refuse to have any contact with us?"

I was unable to explain why. And I would be hard put even now to explain my conduct. It certainly had nothing to do with my attitude toward medicine or prison doctors. But a hunger strike is a hunger strike. I was refusing to eat; so they would have to feed me by force; I would not leave the cell voluntarily for that purpose.

They put the handcuffs on me and dragged me, without beating me, to the medical section. Four guards and an officer went in with me. What with the doctor and the nurses, the room was pretty crowded: it was the same size as our three-man cell. They all tried to talk me into drinking a liquid food preparation. "Why should you make us resort to force? All the hunger-strikers here would rather not be fed through the tube. It still counts as a hunger strike."

Each time the whole procedure made me feel silly. I was not clear in my own mind as to where, at what point, my non-submission ceased to be protest and became sheer mulishness. "You're a stubborn Uke,"⁴ my wife used to say.

On the ninth day of the strike they suggested "nicely" that I drink the starvation ration. It would be so much easier that way, and they would put it in through a tube anyway. But no, I would not drink it. Every day the section warden tried to persuade me to do it, but I would rather have quit striking than drink that liquid from the pan.

Are you going to go take your artificial food? Go like a good boy! If you don't go they'll drag you. If you don't drink the mixture, they'll pour it in through the tube. If you don't open your mouth they'll pry it open for you.

By refusing to eat I put my health and perhaps my life on the line. Why should I quietly go along and open my mouth for them to put the tube in it? Of course I knew that they feed all hunger strikers. But I could not accept that in my own mind. Once I had decided to go hungry, why should I put up with any kind of feeding? So I resisted as best I could. Nevertheless I knew all along that they would get the better of me.

Then there were all kinds of ridiculous details: will you sit on the chair peacefully or will they have to hold you down? Trivial, right? To comply would disgust me as much as being forced. So they held me down on the chair. Eight or ten hands, like a vise, or rather like powerful tentacles wrapped around my weak body. Open your mouth! Or else they will open it for you like a tin can.

I refused. Then someone behind me grabbed my neck with his arm and began to squeeze; someone else pressed on my cheeks, and someone pinched my nose and pulled it upwards. Thank goodness the doctor ordered them to leave my neck alone. They came with the mouth dilatator. I noticed that the tips were bandaged so as not to scratch the lips and gums. At Ashkhabad they did not bother. With my nose shut tight I would have to open my mouth at some point to breathe. I opened my lips a crack and took a swallow of air through clenched teeth. As soon as I did so, in went the dilatator looking for an opening. It hurt my teeth and gums. "Marchenko, open your mouth. Why do you want to make us mad?"

The guard handed the dilatator to the doctor. Finally they laid it aside. They could have jammed it into the mouth, but at the risk of smashing some teeth. And there was a trial coming up. Or did they take pity on my teeth? "Let's put the food in through his nose."

They pulled my head back by the hair and held it steadily in place. I could not move. The doctor had no trouble introducing a thin catheter into my left nostril and injecting the liquid foodstuff by means of a giant syringe. She gave me several injections. Finally it was all over, thank heaven. They released me, but before sending me back to the cell they told me to lie down on the trestle-bed—not so that I would come to, but so that I would not vomit. At this point I did not worry about whether it was voluntary or not: I just lay down.

The next day there was no feeding, and I was delighted. That would most likely mean that the torture would not be a daily affair. But my joy was shortlived. March 8 was a holiday, so the medics apparently had the day off. Starting on the 9th they fed me every day. They no longer tried to do it through the mouth, but stuck the tube right into the nostril. And not a thin one like the first time but three or four times thicker. When they produced it my eyes popped out: even afterwards I could hardly believe that such a huge hose could fit in a human nose. When the tube penetrated into the nasal cavity and they began to push it into the nasopharynx I thought I could feel the cartilage give. It was very painful. I don't know whether they greased it with vaseline—later on, some nurses did and some nurses did not—but it felt like an emery board or a rasp up in there. The pain was intolerable; I could not keep the tears back. Instead of a syringe they now used a funnel, and I could see the thick dark red liquid through the glass, going in slowly as they kept pouring from the pot. When would it all be over? Sometimes there must have been clumps stuck in the tube, for the nurse jiggled it up and down to shake them loose and then pushed it back in deep again. It was hellishly painful. And if that did not work, they would pull the tube out and squeeze the clumps out with their fingers.

It was equally painful when they finally extracted the tube altogether. I had spasms of nausea. They held a towel under my mouth so that if I should throw up it would not splatter all over the room.

When the procedure was over I cheered up and went back to my cell in a good frame of mind: twenty-four whole hours till the next feeding. Back in the cell I began to count the hours till the torture would begin again. At some point I stopped resisting when they took me to the medical room; I went of my own accord and sat down on the chair; I went along with the procedure and held my head back in position because there was nothing else to do. I submitted to the inevitability of torture. But they continued to inject food only by means of a tube through the nose.

In addition to artificial nutriment they tried to give me shots, which I also resisted. Twice the doctor proposed injections (intravenous and subcutaneous, probably glucose and something to strengthen the heart; they do not tell a prisoner what he is getting), and both times I refused. And then the same old routine began: handcuffs, arm-twisting, leg-twisting, and fingers pressing behind my ears to weaken me with pain. I resisted with all my might. Immobilized on the trestle-bed, I tensed my muscles and my skin to keep the needle from going in. The last time, the day before I shipped out, they put some kind of special handcuff on me. It immediately constricted my wrist to such a degree that a spasm went through my arm all the way up to the shoulder, as if from an electric shock. I think I lost consciousness for a minute. They gave me no intravenous injection, but they did give me the subcutaneous one, no doubt. I do not know; I could not feel it. After that, the pain in my arm kept me awake nights. Whether lying down or standing, I could not find a comfortable position for my arm to keep it from aching. To this day I have a dull pain in my shoulders and my fingers grow numb, which makes it hard for me to work. And all because I would not let them give me a shot!

"You're behaving like a wild man," said the doctor indignantly. "We are saving your life and you are driving us to this!"

I agree that I was acting like a savage and a barbarian. What else could the doctor do? She had to use force. For a certain length of time a man can hold out without food, but sooner or later, if nobody intervenes, and if he does not end his hunger strike, he is sure to die. I held out for 45 days in jail—but they did feed me. That doctor tortured me and tortured herself, but she fed me. When I was being transferred, nobody came to my aid, and after eight days I stopped striking. Otherwise I would have died—but there are less agonizing ways and quicker ways to die.

Of course I made it necessary for them to use force on me. Yet I cannot believe that such violence was needed, such a degree of torment (pulling my head back until I went blank, or handcuffing one arm to the chair while the other was bent back over the back of the chair and twisted in again, while the guard pulled the wrist upward and back, practically tying a knot—horribly painful, and pointless). I was in a rage, so naturally the guards lost all sense of proportion, infuriated by my resistance. But the major—the deputy prison commander—was watching the whole thing, and so was the doctor.

I do not believe that four or five powerful guards could not handle me in my weakened state without using torture. After all, they do give injections to thrashing and kicking five-year-olds: usually a single nurse can do the job alone without traumatizing the child. Though I was no child, four heavies could have held me still for half a minute. But a doctor can get angry, too, and I could not blame her since I drove her to it. The upshot was that she did help me and did her professional duty.

But what about a doctor's responsibility when a hunger-striker is allowed to be shipped out? To be transferred with a whole group after 45 days of hunger strike? "What kind of a hunger-striker are you?" said an officer to me at one of the transit prisons. "Something doesn't jibe here. If you were a hunger-striker, they would ship you only with a medic or nurse escorting you." For over a month they threw me out of the rail car into a cell (full of prisoners, with no place to sit or lie down—and no nurse to call) and back into the train again. And the doctor lets a starving man go on a journey like that! It was fully within her power and authority to forbid them to ship me with all the others. No: "Let him croak if he wants to." Then why did she give me her song and dance about that humanitarian profession? "We are saving your life"—yes, so that I would not die on their hands. They forced the food into me so that they could ship me out without even mentioning the strike. Did they save my life with the shot from that shock-handcuff? Far from it: they were simply covering themselves in order to have everything look good on paper in case I should die in transit: blood pressure normal, cardiac activity normal, blood chemistry satisfactory.

"How barbaric!" Yes, barbaric. You would rather have everything look nice and proper: a humanitarian doctor and a grateful prisoner—and then a kick in the rear to topple me into my grave.

A real hunger strike is indeed savage, a form of barbarism, like any self-inflicted torture. Whether the feeding is done peacefully or violently, according to scientific rules or not, it is barbaric nonetheless. You resort to it when there is nothing else left to do.

I counted the days, wondering how long the investigation would drag on. Actually, the investigation was at a standstill; the interrogator did not show up and I just went on sitting. It was perfectly clear, in the first place, that there was nothing to investigate in my case, and, secondly, that it was not being done by the interrogator, who did not even know what had been confiscated when they searched my place. She was not involved in investigation, but rather in putting the paperwork together for the coming attraction. But how much time should that take? By rights, a few days at the most, and yet weeks were passing. That meant that some decision regarding me had not yet been taken. Perhaps it would not come to the worst—but how could that be? I had a brief presentiment of exile, but I could not imagine what grounds would be cited for mitigating the sentence of such a hardened criminal as I, with five offenses on my record. And who would present such arguments to the court? It certainly would not be I. I had made up my mind ahead of time that I would not have my own attorney. To whom would that role be allotted? I rejected the possibility of being sentenced to exile.

Maybe, on the contrary, instead of charging me with violation of parole they would accuse me of something worse, as the KGB had promised. Then the investigation would take months instead of weeks and I would have to serve a term of many years.

Meanwhile the prison officials had not forgotten about me. There were no more heart-to-heart talks; they merely insisted that I end my hunger strike. In our country a hunger strike "does not count" (that is, they pay no attention to it, I know that for a fact). It is a very severe violation of discipline and nothing more. They all piped the same tune—the prison commander, the prosecutor, the doctor and my cellmate.

I hardly noticed myself how weak I was getting. I had constant headaches, but they started before the hunger strike, due to otitis. I began to suffer from intestinal bleeding, but that, too, had happened before; hopefully it would pass. I had trouble walking, particularly up and down stairs.

I noticed that my skin itched, as if from some kind of bites. I scratched myself. Still it itched. As soon as I would lie down on the bed, my skin would itch. At first I thought there could not possibly be lice or bedbugs in that place, with all its automatic devices, tiles and control panels. Out of the question. But my skin continued to itch. I crawled onto the mattress pad and found it—a real cute little prison louse. There is a superstition that lice appear when death is near. Was I already that far gone without knowing it? "Igor, look."

"What, a louse? There are plenty of those in these beds, in every cell."

We called the nurse and told her. She showed no surprise. Still, they took us to the bath and had our things disinfected by heat. They took away our bedding and brought fresh bedding. Back in the cell after the bath, I lay down and the itching began again. Another louse! So even the heat treatment did not work. "No, it does not work," said Igor. These lice are getting smart. They stay out of the heat room. They sit in the clothing issue room while we are bathing. Then they just wander over from the old blankets to the new ones, and back home they go into the cell. This one's an old friend, can't you tell by its face?"

□□□□□

By the end of the month my dossier was ready.

Wow! The file included material from the KGB: a warning, quotes from foreign radio broadcasts, and a denunciation by the forester at Petrishchevo. And all this in connection with a parole violation! So much the better: now I could go on facts and not just guesses; it was not a militia case but a

KGB case. I decided that I would not participate in the legal proceeding but would make a final statement. My main point would be that the trial was retaliation against me for my views and public utterances. And I would talk about slavery and serfdom in the USSR. The dossier itself was loaded with evidence on that score.

My reason for refusing to have a defense attorney was to avoid being limited in my final statement. For the judges that would be a relief, of course: no defense lawyer, and I would not defend myself—so they could kick me lying down. Larisa and I agreed ahead of time that we would apply for permission for her to defend me in court. If they permitted that, the judges were not to be envied. Her logic is so foolproof that any flimsy judiciary arguments would be torn to shreds. But they would not let her in, I was sure of that. So maybe I should have an attorney after all? But the outcome was decided in advance, at any rate, so there was no reason to drag other people into the unpleasantness.

Soon I was presented with the indictment. According to my cellmates, the accusation is usually made known at the same time as the date of the trial, but for some reason they did not tell me when it would begin. I thought that it would open shortly, so I began to get ready. But why prepare? I prepared my final statement, and in order that they would not take it away from me, I wrote it on the back of the bill of indictment. They had no right to confiscate that.

March 31. This morning I was summoned from the cell. The guard told me to put on my jacket, which meant that I would be going out of doors. Where to? To the commander again? Maybe to the prison hosptial? Or will they drive me over to the shrinks? To court!—it dawned on me, and I hastily collected my notes, putting the indictment sheet into my pocket. "No papers!" barked the guard. He took the sheets of paper from my pocket and threw them onto the bed.

On the way I tried to find out where they were taking

me. "No talking!" The guards turned me over to a militia patrol. They ordered me to undress completely; they examined me, searched through all my clothes, and removed every scrap of paper they found, whether anything was written on it or not.

"Where are you taking me?"

"No talking! You'll find out when you get there."

To the courthouse. The snakes. Not only did they not let me know, they took all my papers away to boot. Even the bill of indictment. And like a fool I thought they had no right to do that.

I felt a pain in my heart—maybe from the rough ride, or from excitement, or from anger—and I was growing weak; I felt a chill coming on. When I got out of the paddy wagon I could hardly stand on my legs. "Hands behind your back!"

I did not obey. Immediately they clapped the cuffs on me. The fools took me to court like that. And inside they wanted to remove the handcuffs on the sly, behind the bar, so that no one would notice. But I raised my tethered hands above the partition in order that everyone might see the way they treat their captives. I'm not proud.

My legs would not hold me up; I had to sit down right away. I looked around at the spectators. A lot of them were friends of mine from Moscow, and it was a pleasure to see their smiling faces. I never thought so many people would show up. It is a good four-hour trip from Moscow to Kaluga. They must have left home at the crack of dawn. And there were a handful of visitors from Tarusa. Larisa was there. With whom had she left Pashka? Probably with Iosif Aronovich. All that trouble for Grandpa on my account.

"The court is in session. Will the prisoner please stand!" I did not stand up. The show got under way. I will not go into details of the trial. I have even seen the *samizdat* volume entitled "In the Name of the Russian Soviet Federative Socialist Republic," in which there is given what I consider to be a very detailed and exact account of that trial. I can add

[69]

nothing. So I will merely try to tell how I felt in court. What I felt was closely related to my policy of non-participation in the proceedings.

I had often heard from jurists that it is difficult for a prisoner to adhere to such a mode of behavior and that very few do. It is true that it is not easy: they say all kinds of nonsense about you and you have to shut up. My boss, for instance, testified that I had told her I might go to Moscow for the holidays, whereas in truth what I said was: tell the militia not to worry, I am not going anywhere, I'm staying in Tarusa. I was itching to tell her off, but of course she could remember perfectly well. To the standard question of the judge as to whether the prisoner wished to cross-examine the witness I replied that I would not take part in the court proceedings.

Kuzikov, the Tarusa militiaman, stated that he saw me leave Tarusa by bus. He was lying. He even averted his eyes while he was lying. I would have liked to question him and trip him up, but all I said out loud was: "I am not taking part."

Trubitsyn, the Moscow precinct cop with his square comic-strip face, eyes popping out, made up a whole story: "At such and such a time I carried out my detail.... I had tea.... I wished Marchenko a pleasant holiday...." Lies, lies. Holiday greetings my eye. He could not even look at me; he complained to my wife: "Why does your husband stare at me like a wolf?" I turned around and exchanged glances with Larisa. At that instant she, too, was probably recalling our argument about Trubitsyn. She chided me, saying that I should not regard every functionary as an enemy, that Trubitsyn was a good guy who would not harm a soul and who was just going through his militia routine on his way to retirement. I insisted that this good-hearted pop-eyed fatso would dig a hole and bury the three of us alive if they ordered him to. Look at him now: cheeks puffing out, showing off, and he knows perfectly well that his lies will earn me a good two years in prison camp. Larisa threw me an embarrassed smile, as much as to say: you were right.

"I am not participating." But how hard it is to keep quiet when they stand up one after the other and tell lies! It would be a simple matter to disprove them, to call five witnesses who would state that I did not.... Did not do what? Did not take the bus! And what if I had taken it? Did I try to hijack it? Did I set fire to Tarusa and run away? Did I walk off my duty post? Did I try to ride on the bus without a ticket? No, I just "got on the bus and rode away."

What kind of lies was Trubitsyn telling about me, as the chief witness for the prosecution? "I saw Marchenko walking with his wife and child in the yard.... He was opening the door of his apartment.... I did *not* go for a walk. I did *not* go into the house. But what if I had done so? Had I snatched a kid, was I being tried for kidnapping? Had I broken into someone else's house to steal? Had I disturbed the peace and shouted obscenities outdoors? Or had I maybe got drunk on the glorious October Revolution Day? No, I took a walk with my child and I went into my apartment, and that was the whole story of the crime. Top that if you can.

Why didn't they get Trubitsyn to lay it on even thicker? To say that I called him dirty names, for instance!

Because "there ain't no need." Enough said. I walked with my child and I went into my house--that was enough to keep me in prison for a month and to haul me around in handcuffs. It took an investigator a month to get to the bottom of this dreadful crime--that is, assuming there was an investigation. And for that I went hungry for 33 days. For that my old father-in-law was out there in the courthouse square with his grandchild, worrying what they will do to me, wondering if they will give me a lighter sentence. For that, twenty of my friends, their faces full of pained compassion, were sitting in the Kaluga courtroom, a place they never dreamed of finding themselves in. That was the principal offense for which I would now be sentenced to two years behind barbed wire. That will teach you to take your son out for a walk! You won't be taking walks over there.

And out of a clear blue sky, unexpectedly, a special favor: four years of exile in Siberia. Four years' exile in Siberia for taking a walk with my child in the yard of my house— something I hadn't even done.

"This is an insane asylum!"

"No," says Leonid Brezhnev, First Secretary of the CC CPSU. "This is one of our traditional national rites."

Your rites! *Your* nation, you Soviet Communists! It's not mine. My final statement: "I appeal to everyone in the whole world who can, to assist me and my wife and son to emigrate to the USA. I am continuing my hunger strike.

□□□□□

I was totally worn out from the trial and the two trips in the paddy-wagon there and back. As it turned out, I was not as strong as I thought I was. And now I had the long journey into exile to face. How would I be shipped? Would they splurge on a special escort? Or would they put me into a hospital as long as I was on hunger strike? Then Lord only knows how long it would be before I would see my family again.

I was thunderstruck at the trial by Tatyana Sergeevna's[5] announcement of a solidarity hunger strike. I was going through hell, and here I had dragged another person into the whirlpool. I understood her desperate impulse, but I could not agree with it: must we all be bound by responsibility for each other? What was I to do now? Ten days later I was handed a warm and touching letter from Tatyana Sergeevna: "Don't think that your conduct is the only reason. Not at all.... You should understand the hopelessness of my situation as I understand the hopelessness of yours. Don't be angry and don't worry on my account...." Then she put my mind at rest with these words: "As soon as you start on

[72]

your journey, I will change this situation." That meant that she would end her hunger strike, hopefully soon. Thank God, I could now decide independently as to my own timing.

□□□□□

Taking me to be fed, the guard said: "Why don't you stop your hunger strike? You got exile!"

All the others, too, expected me to end the strike. The prison guards were apparently amazed. After all, a hunger strike "does not count," a hunger strike is a violation of regulations, and on top of that the sentence was mitigated—and how! I should have been sentenced to the penitentiary for my misdeeds and my recalcitrance, but here I was being sent into exile! "You are traveling into freedom."

Indeed, how did things stand now as far as the hunger strike was concerned? I had little strength left, and the strike seemed to make no more sense. Usually a hunger strike is declared in support of some demand. It emphasizes, so to speak, the serious nature and the importance of that demand and readiness to obtain satisfaction at any price, including sacrifice of life. One tries to hold out until the demand is satisfied, but in our country that is practically hopeless, and everybody knows it. A symbolic compromise is in itself an achievement, and even that is a rare occurrence. So the hunger strike served rather to attract attention to the problem, to arouse sympathy and support. Humanists of the Western world, hearken to these appeals! People are sacrificing their health and risking their lives. What is your response?

My hunger strike was not connected with any demands. It was a protest. A political protest, I think. It would be correct to consider this action as having begun not on February 26, when the hunger strike began, but on October 11, the day I announced that I repudiated parole and arrest and would answer by going on a hunger strike. In this way I was not demanding release from responsibility before the law.

The law applied to me was a club wielded by a bandit. What could I ask from a bandit, to say nothing of making demands? My protest would be a reaction to violence, and the more brutal that violence was, the more extreme would be the form which my protest would take.

I have heard it said that the hunger strike (or other forms of violence toward oneself) as a method of protest is a means resorted to by criminals, whereas political prisoners use the hunger strike in connection with some sort of demands. I do not agree. The criminal prisoner mutilates himself both as a sign of protest (for instance, he cuts off his own ear and sticks a tag on it saying "a gift to the CPSU Conference") and by way of demanding something: "Chief, give me some tea, or else I will starve myself to death." Everything depends on what one is demanding or protesting against: that determines whether you are political or criminal or just a fool. Although I did not announce any demands, I must admit that I did allow for the possibility—one chance in a hundred, say—that the publicity would mean that I would not go to prison: my case was embarrassing to the authorities and they might be ashamed. I would have been glad to see it turn out that way. The decision to emigrate, I figured, could increase my chances: the whole parole merry-go-round with everything that followed was staged to force me and my family to leave the country.

I want to explain my actions down to the last detail, whenever I am able to do so, in the hope that the reader will believe me. Therefore I repeat once more: by announcing my desire to emigrate I hoped to influence my fate and the fate of my family. But I did not go on hunger strike for that purpose,* although I did allow that it might have an effect on the outcome by attracting the attention of world opinion to

---

*I am not pleased with my formulation at the trial: "I am staying on hunger strike, and demand to emigrate to the USA." This distorts the issue. I want to emigrate—that is one thing. The hunger strike is another.

my case.

A protest cannot go on indefinitely, however. Exhaustion is its natural limit. After the trial I still had strength, but my forces were almost exhausted. And yet there is another limit, which comes when circumstances seem to have changed (though the violence continues), while somehow becoming stabilized, when the moment of struggle has ceased. Probably the trial should constitute that limit. To prolong the hunger strike now would be to draw attention to myself, to my person, rather than to the heart of the matter. It was time to call it off.

But I could not do that. It would appear as though I were trying to get a better deal. If they had sentenced me to prison camp I might have called off the strike, but I could not do so after receiving a "mild" sentence.

To say that the sentence was mild is stretching a point. To be sure, it was good to know that I would soon see my family, and live without a guard breathing down my neck. Exile is not prison camp. But what was the real upshot? I repudiated a parole status which separated me from my family by an insuperable barrier 200 kilometers long. In exchange— even more crudely and arbitrarily—I was confronted by a barrier extending for 4,000 kilometers. Then the term was half a year (and they would have extended it or fabricated a violation); now it extended for over three years. So why rejoice? And what kind of question is that? "They could have killed you" (that's a line from a joke).

Siberian exile would isolate me from family and friends no less effectively than barbed wire or even the State border. They censor letters, illegally. And at that distance no one has enough time or money. They would isolate not only me, but my wife too, if she came to join me; that was apparently what they counted on. Last but not least, at the place of exile they could do just as good a job as in prison camp of organizing a new case against me: there are plenty of Kuzikovs and Trubitsyns in a Siberian village, and the trial would be kept very quiet. Siberia is not Kaluga.

When I saw my wife on April 1, we somehow managed to exchange ideas on these topics by means of hints and allusions. One cannot have much of a talk in half an hour, sitting in those glass compartments with their junky phones. From both sides you are being overheard by two female sergeants—and somewhere a third set of ears is listening in, no doubt. Larisa began to tell me about Pashka, but tears came to my eyes and I asked her not to talk about my son. I missed him very much. He was very close by, waiting with his grandfather outside the prison gates. And how does Iosif Aronovich feel now? What is he remembering? The Kiev prison, forty years ago, and the six-year-old daughter whom he would not see again until she was seventeen? My father-in-law would soon be eighty. He and I were very much attached to each other. I wondered how he felt now at the sight of his two-year-old grandson.

> Here I sit in the same old cell
> Where my granddad sat long ago,
> Who knows? And the guards will come for me
> As they came for my dad when he was seventeen
> And I'll travel the long long road.

May God save Pashka from the fate of his grandfather, his father and his mother!

April 9. The deadline for appealing the sentence has expired. I did not appeal. On this date the sentence went into force.

That afternoon I was taken to the commander's office. In addition to him, there were also three MVD majors and the parole prosecutor whom I already knew. "Marchenko, is it true that you were beaten when you first came here?" the prosecutor asked. (Probably my wife had registered a complaint after our meeting; certainly the prison commander did not denounce himself. And I had not told anyone else. I said yes, it was true.

"Nobody beat you. Nobody touched you," said one of the majors—the chief of the Kaluga UMZ [possibly the *oblast* administration of the Ministry of Health—*trans.*]—in a tone meant to convince. I had no proof and I had no desire to prove anything. It was too bad that Larisa complained; I had not asked her to do so. The UMZ major also had no proof, but he would not be asked for any. I was not interested in him at this point; I mainly wanted to see what the prison commander would say; he said nothing. I watched him silently fiddling with the levers on his panel, but he did not look up. At least that was something.

(Since then I have learned what he said to my wife in reply to her complaint: "I have heard nothing about any beating." "My husband told me he spoke to you...." "I verified that and it was not confirmed." "But you just said you knew nothing about it! How did you check—did you ask the people who did the beating?" "Your husband was examined by the doctor, who found no traces of any beating." Another lie! Nobody examined me. I had filed no complaint, and he knew that. "I realize that I have no evidence to support my complaint. I told you about this instance so that you could be on the alert: others are probably being beaten, too." "Nobody beat your husband.")

Next question: about the papers taken away before the trial. Again the prison commander said nothing, and the administration major argued that no papers were confiscated. "But I was taken empty-handed into court! I said so to the judge, and the audience knows it."

"Then maybe Marchenko himself left the papers in his cell on purpose. Tell the escort guard to come here." At this point the prison commander broke in. He could not remember who was on duty and had no way of finding the guard who had escorted me to the trial.

The prosecutor could see that the case was not clear-cut, and that they should be careful about accusing me of lying lest they should make a slip and fall into their own trap. So they treaded water for a whole hour. "Why didn't you tell the escort? Oh, he took away your papers, too, did he? What do you mean, you did not know the date of the trial? You were told when it would be!"

"No, I wasn't."

"That's not possible." Then, to the prison commander: "He was informed, wasn't he?" The prison commander remained silent. He knew that I had not been told. The major from the special section *(spetschast)* nodded: "I told him myself." The prosecutor, reassured, asked for confirmation in writing. But there was no document; they did not have my signature; nor the signature of witnesses in the event of my refusal to sign.

Once again the conversation turned to the question of the confiscated papers. "Maybe they were not taken away after all?" "This is not the same thing as the beating. Not taken away? All the people in the courtroom saw how they brought the papers in and gave them to me toward the end of the trial." "What!" exclaimed the administration major with a start. "Then you have them on you? Comrades!" With a sweeping gesture he addressed his colleagues: "Did you hear that? He has the papers, they were given back to him! This man is spreading dirt and we sit here discussing it. They gave him the papers back!"

The prosecutor and the prison commander tried to stare him down, to keep him from getting carried away, but he would not be dampened: "We just handed you a telegram from Jamaica!" (That was true, I got a telegram of sympathy and support.) "You were given that telegram in person. And as it turns out you got your papers back! And you.... At this point he finally became aware of the prosecutor's warning glance. He sat with his mouth hanging open, looking from one to the other in bewilderment. The issue, by the way, was a serious one: taking the bill of indictment away from the accused consitutes a violation of his right to defense, and that is sufficient justification for the case to be reviewed. How could the administration major not know that? He, too, had a diamond-shaped insignia on his uniform, which meant he had a higher education. Be all that as it may, in spite of awkward moments everything was smoothed over. My wife was notified that I had not been beaten and that my papers had been on me during the trial. And this after all the spectators had been witnesses to the contrary! If the prosecutor himself was a liar, how could one blame poor Kuzikov?

And how about my honest major? I was triumphant. My theory concerning pigs in pig slots proved to be correct. Towards evening I received further confirmation: they handed me an order forbidding a personal meeting with my wife, signed by "the commander of SIZO no. 1, Major N.V. Kuznetsov." But somehow my perspicacity did not make me very happy.

April 12. Aerospace Day. It was celebrated like a royal holiday in Kaluga, "the historical cradle of space flight." Every loudspeaker in town blasted forth on this theme from early morning on—and there were plenty of loudspeakers: one in every cell, and one in the courtyard. Soviet bragging and smugness over space exploits always annoy me. I get all wrought up like a little boy. What do they have to be so proud about? The local newspaper writes that some city transportation routes have been closed down due to bad road conditions in spring weather; from neighboring areas, people can hardly get to this cosmic cradle on tractors; but no, they are the first and the best in the world!

The feeding today was about two hours earlier than usual. The day before, there had been a physical examination: did that mean they were getting me ready to be shipped out? Lying on my bed after being force-fed, I did not know which nauseated me more—the accursed tube or the triumphant tone of the radio announcer. I wanted to think about other things, but I could not, probably because I was so angry. They broadcast interviews, reports, reminiscences about Gagarin, all flavored with loud optimistic music. There was a playback of on-the-spot coverage dated April 12, 1961, from the cosmodrome. At that time, at age 23, I had been confined at the Semipalatinsk transit prison on the way to Taishet.

Through space noise and crackle came Gagarin's voice: "Let's go!" The door of the cell swung open. On the threshold stood a smiling guard with my identity card in his hand. He said: "Okay, Marchenko, let's go!" I gathered my things together—soap, toothpaste, socks and an English grammar book.

□□□□□

In the prison isolation cage I was turned over to the escort guard, searched, and questioned: "Can you make it to the vehicle?" So they knew they had a hunger striker on their hands. "Do you have any objections to being transferred long distance?" I replied that I had been on hunger strike for 45 days. I did not answer any other questions. "Here is your ration for the road." "I will not accept it."

The first sergeant accompanying the vehicle took the ration, and I was locked up in the tiny compartment in back: iron sides and an iron door with a tiny peephole. I was alone —thank the Lord for little blessings. Maybe Major Kuznetsov, looking out of his office window at the departing paddy-wagon, gloated: "He's gone!" And maybe the prison doctor was giving a sigh of relief: "At last he's on his way!"

I also told the train escort detail that I had been hunger-striking for 45 days. "What was that? What did you say?" said the chief escort. The prison officer whispered something in his ear and he stopped asking questions. He yelled: "Get into that boxcar, make it snappy!" The first seargeant tried to shove the food ration at me, but I wouldn't take it. I was put in a three-man compartment in the boxcar; a second man from Kaluga came in after me. The third occupant, who was already there, had been traveling since Voronezh. The Kaluga prisoner shoved a bundle at me right after they had pushed him into the car. "Are you Marchenko? The sergeant told me to give you this. It's your ration."

"I will not accept the package. I am on hunger strike."

Realizing he had stepped right into it, this guy got apologetic: "F... it all anyway, if he had told me the story, I would not have played along."

□□□□□

I had often been on shipment from prison to prison, and I was worried as to how I would take the pleasures of the journey in my condition. But I had confidence in my forces and my perseverence, and I had every intention of prolonging my hunger strike throughout the trip and into exile. Also I had seen hunger-strikers on such trips and had heard about them, and I knew that no matter how bad things are, the guards somehow manage to keep them going and prevent them from dying. Normally they separate them from the others, whether on the road or in the transit prisons. I could not imagine beforehand how hard it would be to stick it out this time.

The route by which they shipped me from Kaluga was as follows: via Kalinin to Yaroslavl (transit stop); Perm (transit stop); Sverdlovsk (transit stop); Novosibirsk (transit stop); Irkutsk (transit stop); and Chuna, the end of the line. We spent a total of almost a month at the transit points as against some ten days on the road. Sometimes we would stand on sidings for eight hours or so while the car got shifted and hooked up, with all of the prisoners locked up inside. In all, I was under way for a month and eight days.

In the accompanying documents there was no mention of my hunger strike; I made repeated verbal statements to that effect, however, and yet during the entire time—before I stopped striking and afterwards—not a single individual from the medical personnel came over to see about me, and no concessions were made to me because of my condition. Everywhere—at the transit points, in the rail car—I was thrown in with all the others and subjected to the same routine and discipline. I was part of the prison crowd. That meant being jammed into overflowing paddy-wagons, standing up for hours in solitary, lying on cement floors (if there is room left in transit cells, going upstairs and down and across the hall when the roll is called, into the bathhouse and out for a walk, come on, come on, be quick about it! Take that mattress upstairs to your cell, turn this mattress in, get the lead out of your big behinds! Don't keep everybody waiting!)

Since I had been forbidden to see my wife before departure, I had no canteen or canteen cup for the water I would need en route. Thus, I was able to wet my parched mouth three times a day from the container the guard brought around. This state of affairs had one advantage: I did not have to suffer from stop to stop, nor hear the guard say, in answer to a request to go to the toilet: do it in your boots. On the third day of the journey I felt I was nearing the end of my rope.

April 14. At Yaroslavl they unloaded us from the train and an escort from Yaroslavl took the gang over. The new guards did a count and a name check against their own lists. I announced to them that I had been on hunger strike for the past 47 days. "There is no hunger striking around here," was the response.

The only two benches in the transit reception room were full; new arrivals had to stand. They packed us in so tight, we had to stand shoulder to shoulder. The room was so stuffy and full of smoke that you could hardly distinguish faces. I probably would have keeled over if a companion who worried about me had not got someone to give me his seat on a bench.

After four hours of that ordeal they took us to the bath. I did not have enough strength to wash myself; and I just sat there while the others bathed. After the bath—back to the standing room, but not for long this time. They finally gave me a prison mattress with a pillow and other supplies, and took me to a cell. Thank God it was a small three-man cell with only two of us in it. I lay down right away.

In the prison I stated once more that I was on a hunger strike. My declaration met with the same retort as before: "No hunger strikes here!"

I wrote out a formal statement addressed to the prison commander declaring that I was on hunger strike. I handed it to the officer on duty, who refused to take it. "What is this about?" he asked.

"Hunger strike."

"You are announcing that officially?"

"No. I am already on a hunger strike, I have been since the day of my arrest, which makes 47 days now."

The officer went away without taking the statement. He returned shortly and said: "I looked at your file and there is no mention of a hunger strike in it. We do not recognize hunger strikes here."

That really made me flip. After getting a little rest for an hour or so I began to insist that my statement be accepted. I tried to hand it to the guards and to duty officers and kept asking for a doctor or a medic to come around. I hammered on the door with my fists. My fellow prisoner did his share of banging: there was no glass in the cell window, and air came through cracks in the door as well; we sat smack in the middle of the draught, shivering and clacking our teeth. It was mid-April and quite cold.

The section warden finally showed up. My companion demanded to be put into a normal cell; I demanded to see a doctor and to have someone accept my written statement. Why was I nursing this piece of paper like that? What exactly did I want? I insisted on seeing a doctor, but why? To be fed by force? No, I honestly did not want that. I felt no hunger at all and had no desire to eat. I was not going out of my way to be tortured; suffering gave me no satisfaction. (I do not mean this ironically. But I hear there are such cases.) Did I just want to keep myself going? Actually, no. On the third day of the trip I was already very weak, and I must say that that is a disgusting state to be in—both physically and morally. I could sense my strength waning by the hour; knowing that sooner or later the moment would come when I could no longer get up, I started wishing for that moment to come. I did not think about what might happen beyond that point. I could stop the hunger strike, but I was afraid of killing myself that way, since I did not know the right way to go about it. Or I might lose consciousness, thereby freeing myself from responsibility for myself—a base thought, but in my weakness I wanted very much to get rid of the burden of all efforts, including moral responsibility. On the other hand, by becoming totally exhausted I would not have to get up or move. I could just go on lying there; I would be unable to get up and nobody could do anything about it.

But for the time being I was apparently able to move around. And so I had to drag myself along with the others, who were strong and healthy. If they had acknowledged my hunger strike, they would not have forced me to run up and down the corridors and from one transit prison cell to another, or compelled me to get up for head check. I could have just continued to lie there peacefully. I wanted them to leave me alone and stop bothering me. "Here is my hunger strike statement. Take it!"

"We have no hunger strikers here."

Evidently the hardest thing for me to endure was the attitude of indifference toward me—not toward me as Anatoly Marchenko, but toward me as a human being. "No hunger strikers"—and that's that, and what you are doing is not a hunger strike. It is very simple: whether you eat your dinner or throw it away is your own business. I would not even have minded so much the lack of concessions or alleviations, or objected to confinement in punishment cells, if only they had admitted to themselves that the man whom they were driving so hard, whom they forced to get up and run around, was a starving man, who would finally collapse and die. But no: "We have no hunger strikers here."

"Take my statement!"

"Calm down."

"I want to see the doctor."

"Just wait, the doctor will be around."

But the doctor did not come around. Or else he might just look in through the feeding bin and ask what the trouble seems to be.

"Hunger strike.... I've had no bowel movement for five days. I need a laxative."

"All right, just wait."

But he would go away and not come back.

During the first night in Yaroslavl I did not sleep. I lay in a state of semi-consciousness until reveille. The next night, at midnight, they came to get me for shipping out. I was too weak to carry my mattress to the supply room, so I left the cell empty-handed. The guard cursed, pulled me by the arm and threw me back into the cell so hard that I hit the wall. But fortunately my cell-mate came to my aid and carried the bedding out for me.

Prisoners being shipped out were herded into the transit reception room. Here we had to spend the rest of the night standing up: there were no benches to sit on. In the morning the rations for the road were handed out—herring and bread. I refused to accept mine and said I was on strike. "How long have you been on hunger strike?"

"49 days."

"49 days, and you're still alive?" The captain was amused. "Ha, ha, ha! Pretty tough, aren't you? Ha, ha, ha!" The captain's huge frame shook with laughter, his belly bobbing up and down. I was furious. I felt humiliated and powerless.

About forty minutes later the captain showed up again at the cell door. His giant figure filled the doorway so that I could hardly see the guards behind him. "Where is the hunger striker? Come over here!"

With great effort I got up off the floor and squeezed my way through the room to the door, where I told the captain that I was the hunger striker. He stood with his hands behind his back and looked me over. "Come on, striker, want to wrestle?" The captain laughed and the men behind him roared. It was quiet in the room.

I stepped back a little in order not to lose my temper. I brooded over this episode for a long time, and I remembered it again and again later, when I was far from Yaroslavl and had ended my hunger strike. Why hadn't I spit in that swine's face? Or, rather, why did I control myself? It would be interesting to know what would have happened to me if I had spit at him or thrown something. A fight? A trial?

April 18. At dawn we arrived at Perm. Here again I made my declaration to the escort guard: I am on a hunger strike, I have not eaten for 50 days.

"Where is your medical escort?"

"How am I supposed to know?"

"Something is wrong here. If you were on hunger strike, no escort guard would take you without an accompanying doctor or medic."

As usual, the paddy-wagon was stuffed full, and as the last comer I had no room. The prisoner in front of me managed to squeeze himself halfway in, but I was left out. They kept shouting at me to get a move on. Seeing that I did not try very hard, two guards held on to the door and pushed me with their knees into the solid mass of prisoners. After forcing me in, they closed the grill door, and my jacket got caught in it. I hung like that for about an hour, while they loaded the other vehicles, drove through the town and stood in the prison courtyard. I do not know whether I was conscious the entire time.

That day I presented a written statement regarding my hunger strike to officers on duty on two occasions, and both times the piece of paper fluttered down to the floor. "You got your ration? You ate it, didn't you? So what's all this about a hunger strike?"

The other prisoners sympathized with me and were indignant at the prison guards. My companion from Yaroslavl told them: "I was in the same cell with him and we sat together on the same bench in the boxcar for two days, and I know that he never put so much as a crum in his mouth. And he never took his ration either."

"Can't you tell by looking at him?" said another prisoner.

But no one understood why I was being so stubborn. "You're not going to impress them." "If you die they'll be happy." "There ain't no justice." And other remarks like that. All of them tried to persuade me in a friendly way to drop the whole thing.

The time had come to end the hunger strike. I decided that I would do so the next day. But today they took all new arrivals to the doctor for examination. (For some reason this was called a "commission.") Six men were taken into the office at a time and asked a few questions; there was no examination at all.

"Any complaints? No lice?"

I said that I had been on hunger strike for 51 days.

"And where is your doctor?"

"He's in Kaluga, at the medical section of the prison."

"You should be under medical escort all the way to your final destination. When were you fed the last time?"

"On the 12th, the day I got shipped out."

"Today is the 18th." She looked at me dubiously. "When did you have a bowel movement?"

"On the 9th. Give me a laxative."

"My job is checking the transit prisoners through. Somebody else is in charge of treatment." But I never saw "somebody else," and I never saw her again either.

For a whole day they took us to the baths, checked and rechecked us, put us in groups and herded us into the transit reception rooms. Many of the men I had been traveling with were sent to the "chemical works"—apparently the same thing was true at previous transit points as well. The compartment walls were scrawled over with farewell inscriptions: "Eighteen men from Grozny left for the chemical works today"—followed by the date. "Twenty-two men from Kishinev left for the BAM"[6] —and the date.

In the cell, where I was put toward evening, there were about 25 people, all "chemists" and prisoners sentenced to exile. Unlike the prison camp inmates, each of us was issued two bedsheets, the first time I had encountered such luxury. But four men, including me, were left without cots, so we had no place to spread our sheets. We four got wooden boards to put on the floor for the night; at six a.m. they took them away again, and we had no place to lie down. Of course there is always the bare floor.

April 19. As it turned out, it was not so easy to stop. In the morning I refused food again, tried unsuccessfully to hand my statement to the duty officer, and asked to see the doctor. The guard said that the doctor would come; but a prisoner with a big infected sore on his leg seemed to know better: "Oh, sure, the doctor will be around—maybe once in a week, and even then you have to fight to get to see him."

I waited for the doctor anyway. What else could I do? I mainly wanted to lie down, but I had no place to lie, and the doctor did not show up.

Today was the 52nd day of my hunger strike, and I had been in transit for a week. How did I manage to keep going? That captain was right: I was a tough one. If only I could pass out! Then I would know that I had reached the limit and would stop the hunger strike. And then perhaps they would let me lie down and rest. It looks as though I still expected to find some sort of humane treatment in my own country. For the time being I was able to lie down for a bit on the beds of my cellmates.

Dinner was brought around and I refused again. But why? No, I was still determined to have my strike officially recognized. I was too feeble to kick or knock on the door: all that I produced by such efforts was a faint scratching noise, not enough to attract the attention of guards in a transit prison, who are used to much worse racket. My cellmates then fixed me up with a battering ram: they moved the table to the door and on it put a bench upside down, so that one could bang on the door with the bench by sliding it back and forth. For many of them this was a source of entertainment as a change from the drab routine of confinement, and they were curious to see how it would all end. Some of them egged me on and some warned me: "You better cut that out, or else they'll drag you out and throw you into the punishment cell." Only the day before, they had done that to somebody; that was not unusual around here.

Well, let them punish me if they want to, I thought. I didn't care any more. I rammed at the door, making a loud noise each time the bench banged against it. The hall guard came up, looked through the peephole, saw the battering ram and started to shout and curse. I continued to bang, like a robot. The guard went away. After a while there was a rattle at the lock. Everyone in the cell was silent, ready for trouble. Someone whispered: "If they tell you to go out, don't go." Someone else pulled me away from the door. But then the door opened and on the threshold stood three guards, one of whom pointed a finger at me.

"Come out," he said.

Two or three fellows raised their voices in my defense. The guard pointed at them and said: "And you come out, too."

The voices died down. I stepped out into the ill-lit corridor, expecting the first blow to fall. But nobody hit me. At the wall to one side I noticed an elderly major with a blue diamond-shaped insignia on his uniform and an armband reading "assistant commander on duty."

"What have you got there," asked the major. I handed him the statement. He read it—and took it! "I will give this to the commander. You will see the doctor." I was put back into the cell, to the amazement of the others. Two hours later they took me out into the hall again, to the same major. He had my statement in his hand. "The commander will not see you. How can you be on hunger strike? You are not serving a prison sentence, you are on your way into exile, where you will be a free man. You can do your complaining when you get there. We here no longer have anything to do with you and we are not going to look into your statements. That's all."

"Will I see the doctor?"

"What do you want from him?"

Actually, what did I want?*

"I need a laxative."

"I will tell the medical section."

"I have no place to lie down."

The major turned to the hall guard and ordered him to find room for me. The guard said: "And where am I supposed to find it? All of the cells are overcrowded. There is more room in here than anywhere else."

Back in my cell, I still had no place to lie down. No doctor appeared, not even the nurse, who occasionally brought pills around to the cells for headaches and stomachaches. Taps.

*Comment by the wife of Anatoly Marchenko: In my opinion my husband wanted only one thing: compassion. That alone would have made things easier for him in those difficult days when he was getting weaker by the hour and felt to-totally helpless. He was looking for compassion rather than for concrete assistance. And why from the doctor? From whom else? From a guard, or a prosecutor? A doctor wears a white smock and has a red cross on his case—obsolete symbols of

April 20. In the night I awoke on my floor board with a sharp pain in my stomach. I was shaking and I had a dull pain in my heart. The stomach pain spread through my entire abdomen—first spasmodically and then, toward morning, more evenly. I did not get up for reveille, but there was no problem. I got a place on a lower berth temporarily and lay down on my stomach, trying not to move because I was in such pain. I had stopped thinking about my hunger strike, about whether to end it or to prolong it; I no longer tried to get my statement accepted and no longer demanded to see the doctor. There I lay, and was happy when the pains subsided somewhat.

---

service in the name of charity.

Anatoly categorically rejects my interpretation: "After all, I knew what kind of people I was dealing with." Obviously he knew. Yet I still think that I am right. In weakness and suffering everyone of us looks for a helping hand, a kind voice, a word of compassion. But our life does not exactly abound in charity. The Sister of Mercy has been replaced by the medical nurse, whose function it is to handle a needle with skill and keep track of the pills. There is no one left to turn to for spiritual support—certainly not the Party organizers. From our earliest school days our education runs counter to the notion of pity. "Do not take pity. Do not humiliate a person by feeling sorry for him."

That is the main difference between penal confinement in Old Russia and in our day: in the old prisons and exile colonies, prisoners could expect some charity and compassion, but today they do not. In former days there were three lawful channels through which charity flowed: the church, the doctors (including sisters and brothers of mercy), and the natural kindheartedness of the people, who were brought up in that spirit by the church. That spirit was not always able to understand each person and to bring about his regeneration, but it alone had the power to penetrate the hardened souls of criminals who had cut themselves off from the world. It is evident that prisoners in those days sought charity, for when they had eaten their fill of prison food they went begging in Christ's name and received alms on holidays. Somehow this did not humiliate them; on the contrary, sometimes it elevated them, lifted them out of their degradation.

In our modern penal system there is no room for pity, for kindness, for sympathy. All good things and special favors are meted out on a mechanically calculated basis: the prisoner is expected to prove that he is worthy and deserving, to earn what he gets. Even the sick are not always officially listed as such; even mothers fail to be included in amnesties.

But how can a prisoner hope to find charity when it does not exist in everyday life?

"All out for exercise!" I heard the command as though it came from far away. I heard the men in my cell filing out into the hall. I did not get up. "Whatcha doin' there? Out!" the guard, a young Caucasian, yelled as he yanked my jacket off me.

"I can't get up."

"You can't, huh? Where's yer doctor's excuse?"

"I haven't seen any doctor."

"Git outta there." And he jerked me from the cot. But instead of getting up I dropped right back down onto the bunk. The Caucasian swore and went away. The other prisoners were lined up in the hall and they had to be taken out for their walk. Now I hoped that I would be left in peace, and I began to work myself into a comfortable position in bed. I got settled and relaxed. And my pains grew less acute, though my chill got worse. Then two guards—the Caucasian and another one—burst into the cell and without a word pulled me off the bunk and hauled me to the door. I was unable to stand up, or rather to move my legs, and they kicked me in the legs with their boots. Was I really incapable of walking, or was my weakened body reacting subconsciously to their violence? I don't know.

At the threshold I tried to resist. In response I received the customary treatment—arm twisted behind my back and a lateral kick in the belly. When I came to, I was on the floor of the corridor. I looked up and right in front of my eyes was a pair of box-calf boots. Someone was holding my arm and looking for my pulse; someone else was telephoning. "And suppose he dies here on our hands? Take him to the hospital and do what you want with him, but I refuse to be responsible for him. If he dies...."

I wasn't exactly delighted to hear that. The guard replaced the receiver and said to his companion: "The doctor is on his way, let's get him back into that cell." They patted my cheeks and shook me, but more gently this time. They tried to pick me up, but I collapsed right back to the floor;

my legs would not hold up under me. Then the guards took me by the arms and legs, dragged me into the cell, tossed me onto the bunk and departed, leaving the cell door open. I lay there with my face down, curled up with my legs pressed against my stomach to ease the pain. But I was still in prison and the guard was responsible for me. He came back in and turned me over onto my side with my face toward the door.

"It hurts me to lie like that," I said. He told me to stay that way and he left.

After a little while I heard someone come into the cell and pause without approaching the bed. I opened my eyes. A woman in white was standing about two meters away from me; she did not come closer.

"What seems to be the trouble?"

"Hunger strike, 53 days."

"You should have a medical escort..." she said, and other things to the usual effect.

"I need a laxative."

"All right, I'll give you one. When were you fed last?"

"Before shipping out, eight days ago."

"And nothing since then?" She asked me when I had last relieved myself, and I told her on the ninth. She opened her medical bag with a red cross on it and took out a small packet. Suddenly she looked at me and put the packet back in the bag. "You can't have this now. A laxative would only weaken you further."

She went away. The door slammed shut, then just as noisily swung open again. In came a guard together with an officer—a colonel or lieutenant colonel. "Get up!" I did not stir or lift my head.

"Stand up! You heard me."

"I am bedridden."

"The commanding officer is here in front of you and you think you can go on lying there? I said get up."

"Why don't you lie down, too?"

"Wha-a-at?! I can throw you into punishment cell!"

[93]

"He can do that just as well as you can," I retorted, pointing at the guard.

The officer paced the floor of the cell and then came toward me once more: "What are you in for?" He used the familiar "thou."

"Don't get familiar with me," I said.

"I use the polite form of address with my best friends, not when I am talking to criminals." What a fool he was!

He came closer and I could smell vodka on his breath. "Hunger strike or no, we're sending you out with the next load."

The other prisoners, back from their exercise, were already milling about in the hall. They were not admitted to the cell until the officer had gone out. "The big boss," I heard them say when they came in. I had asked for an appointment to see him and my request was turned down; now it was he who had come to see me.

□□□□□

All day I lay on the bunk. Nobody disturbed me. After taps I crawled over onto my floor board. My stomach pains had subsided altogether, my chills were less severe; only my heart still ached.

My written statement was a thing of the past. And I did not want anything from the doctor. I myself could not understand why I was churning about or what it was I was after. I lay there without moving; I was peaceful and I needed nothing else. I should have done this long before: I should have refused to get up even if they killed me. Now I began to think. Let's see. I was being sent from Kaluga on a prison trek for 4000 km. They sent me out hungry, after a month and a half on hunger strike; not only was I shipped out without a medical escort, which apparently is obligatory in such cases, but also without any notation of the hunger strike in the documents accompanying me. It was hardly credible that the Kaluga prison officials and prison physician should have assumed such a responsibility without having been so instructed by whoever it was who manipulated my fate behind the scenes.

What was the plan? Did they count on my dying en route? Or did they think that I would bring my hunger strike to a close? Even if I had stopped striking, that would have been no guarantee that I would not perish. They would inform my wife of my death, attributing it to whatever cause they chose, once they had made up their own minds that "he dug his own grave, let him lie in it," and that "a dog dies a dog's death." And not only would no one bear any responsibility, but no one would feel the slightest guilt.

What do I care anyway? And yet it would be a shame to let myself be killed off so easily, unavenged, and let them get away with it. What is more, I had no intention of dying.

Three months before I was arrested, my wife urged me not to go on hunger strike, or at least not for an unlimited period. She bargained with me: "Two weeks is enough. Well, maybe three weeks. You are not making any demands, and as a declaration of protest that is plenty." I laughed and said I would be able to hold out for several months and would definitely quit before reaching a critical point. I had no desire to die.

How long would I be able to endure without artificial feeding, that is, if they did not pump me full at all, from the start of the hunger strike? Probably for about a month and a half or two, or maybe even longer—not while traveling, of course, but if I stayed in one place. I could be wrong. Now, however, would I be able to go on without eating? Who knows? I have heard that a person on hunger strike may die not from starvation but from heart paralysis. So at what point would an extra load on the heart, such as running, breathing bad air, being pushed and crowded and so on, be the last straw? As it was, my heart was hurting and aching, though it had been perfectly healthy before. Furthermore, a guard might haul off with his fist, thinking he was dealing with a healthy person, and that's the end of that. Such a thing might happen at any time.

If they were to leave me alone, and in a less crowded cell, I could have continued to go hungry. For three more days, perhaps. Then I would have had to stop striking anyway, for I really did not want to die, particularly since that would make them happy. I probably should have ended the strike during the early stages of the journey, say, at Yaroslavl. But like a fool I got all worked up when they said "we have no hunger strikers here." And it never seemed to be the right time: boxcars, compartments, paddy-wagons, baths, "I refuse to accept the ration"—in the midst of all that there was no occasion to reflect and make a sensible decision. To reorient oneself psychologically, one must have peace, and not simply grab a bite on the run after not eating for so long.

53 days. That's enough. Tomorrow morning I will end my strike.

April 21. My decision meant that this morning I would take my ration—half a loaf of black bread. The problem was what to do with it. I did not know how to come out of a hunger strike and there was no one I could ask. And even if I had known how to go about it, the knowledge would have made no difference. Scientific advice would have been of no avail since I was limited to the prison diet.

For the moment my ration remained untouched. For breakfast they give out a ladleful of kasha—I would begin with that. I don't know what kind of grain they made that kasha out of, and I am not about to guess. Prisoners call it "kersey," because it is coarse and scratches the throat. It has a bluish color. I chewed on that porridge practically all morning, chewing and chewing till it turned into glue in my mouth. I began to salivate soon after I began to chew. I strained it through my teeth a few times and then managed to swallow it with difficulty. The food itself left me indifferent; I was interested only in the process of eating, having lost the habit. After the kasha I ate about 100 g of the soft part of the bread with equal caution, and sipped hot water with my sugar ration. For about two weeks I did not eat the cabbage soup *(shchi)* they handed out for lunch, and I stayed away from the sprats. That meant that during the rest of the trip I ate practically nothing but bread. The ration for prisoners in transit consisted of bread, sprats or herring, and 20 g of sugar per day. In the evening I ate the liquid part of the fish soup.

I must say that the chow is better these days than it was five years ago. The food at the transit points is easier to digest; the sugar ration has been increased by 5 g a day. It used to be 15 g. Do you think that's not much? This is a 30 percent improvement under the five-year plan.

My appetite began to come back on the second day and, as time went on, I got hungrier and hungrier. I had to keep myself from consuming the whole day's ration all at once, and I was ashamed to catch myself wanting to ask for a second helping of soup. Asking for seconds in prison is no disgrace. Whether you can get them is another question. One thing I did know was the danger of eating too much right after a period of starvation, and so I kept to a semi-starvation diet for quiet a while. That is not hard to do when one is a prisoner.

□□□□□

On that same day the prosecutor made his monthly rounds. The "big boss"—the prison commander—showed him our cell: "These men are free prisoners *(volnyye).* Two are on their way to exile and all the others are 'chemists.'"

"Any questions for the prosecutor?"

Everyone had the same question: when were we going to be shipped out of there? The majority had already been there for three weeks.

[97]

Exiled prisoners in transit get credit against their sentences at the rate of one to every three days. The "chemists" leave prison camp or courthouse under a "chemical" amnesty (that is, they are really "free" or amnestied; yet they still travel with other prisoners under guard. And they get no credit for time in transit. They envy the exiles.

The prosecutor's visit was a form of distraction. No one took it seriously. The prison commander acted like a clown; the prisoners laughed when the prosecutor came and again when he left. All parties were satisfied with the show.

April 22. I was already in Sverdlovsk. Though I was no longer starving, that part of the journey was just as hard on me as the preceding stages. The same crowded paddy-wagons and boxcars, the same hour-long standing in transit reception compartments. When it came time to bathe I was already exhausted and could not wait to get to a cell and lie down.

Cell number 11 at the Sverdlovsk transit prison has to be seen to be believed. It is a huge hall, about 120 square meters. In the middle, about a meter and a half or two meters away from the wall, stands a two-tiered bunk bed structure measuring 10 meters by 4 meters. The only way to get into bed is by going all the way around. The rest of the room is occupied by a long table with benches and by the "toilet."

I spent four days in that room. When I was there it contained 163 men. How did we all fit in? In the daytime it was not so bad: a man takes up less space when he is sitting down. But at night! They lay on the bunks, on the table, under the table. There was no room to pass, because they lay on the floor, too. They did not actually lie down: with only a couple of meters or so between the bunks and the walls there was not enough space to lie down all the way. You had to either bunch yourself up like a pretzel or lean sitting up against the wall with legs out. I got a reserved seat in the pretzel department. I had to be careful not to stretch out while sleeping so as not to kick my foot in the face of somebody sleeping under the bunks. And there was always the risk of someone stepping on me on his way to the toilet during the night. Only two toilet bowls were provided, which was too few.

For roll call they chased everybody out into the hall, lined us up in rows of three each, and counted the rows. The guard read all the announcements through a megaphone, his voice rising above the din of shouting and cursing that filled the cell at all times. If any one man had to be summoned, this was done by the grapevine method: "Petrov is wanted outside." "Tell Petrov." "Where is Petrov?" "Is that Petrov?" "Hey, Petrov"—then you get a poke in the ribs: "Are you Petrov? Oh no? Then pass it on."

When the bread was brought around, you had to hustle, or you would end up without any ration. The soup man put the authorized number of bowlfuls into the feed-bin. Some of the more clever prisoners would wait near the door for lunch, eat their soup, and scamper back among the others before your turn came, say the 150th. The soup man would count out: "One hundred sixty-three!" and slam the bin shut. So you and the rest would go without lunch.

You had to look out for your footgear even more than for your feet. Somebody might step on your foot, but they might walk away with your boots and you'd never see them again. And not only boots. They would try to get any loose clothing off your back that you had brought from the outside; they would steal it or try to get it in exchange for prison camp rags. First they would come up to you real friendly like: "Hey, pal, let's trade." And quite seriously they would suggest you give up a sweater or a decent suit in exchange for a torn *bushlat* jacket that had been issued in prison. Then came the hints and persuasion. You might resist, but as soon as you fell asleep they would take everything and you would get nothing in exchange. My sweater and foreign-made boots attracted great interest, and guys came up to me "real friendly like." At night I had to sleep with one eye open, so to speak, worrying about my belongings. When

I undressed I folded the sweater under my back and put the boots under my legs—you can't sleep with your boots on. One time a group got a card game going right next to me; the loud talking did not bother me; but through my dozing I felt something pull at my boot. I stopped and started again. I opened my eyes a tiny bit and saw that one of the card-players was trying to yank my boots out from under my legs. I raised one leg up as if in my sleep and braced it against the bunkbed frame; then I waited for the guy to reach under for the boots, at which point I would pin him down by the neck with my leg. But he looked suspiciously from the boots to the raised leg, glanced over at my face to see if I was sleeping, exchanged glances with the others, and walked back to the table followed by the other card-players. Thank goodness there was no fight. These guys, called "sixers" *(shesterki)*, worked for professional thieves: two young ones in the cell, around 26 years old and built like wrestlers, would work a newcomer over with friendly talk, and then let the "sixers" move in. After that incident they left me alone. Perhaps they guessed that I had some experience with prison camps. Yet they could have just robbed me blind, for I was too feeble to fight. These thugs, however, usually do not rob openly.*

Cell number 11 contained convicts, "chemists" and exiles. There were more "chemists" than anybody else, since in March the regular "chemical" amnesty had been declared, and prisoners were being funnelled in load after load through Sverdlovsk to Tyumen *oblast*. But the exile prisoners (for the most part alimony-defaulters: "What are you in for?" "For my golden eggs!") and the penal colonists were being shipped mainly to the BAM project in Irkutsk *oblast*.

All across the cell walls the prisoners had scrawled the long transport route from Moscow to Vladivostok. All the

_____

*In Nakhodka, a cellmate told me, they steal openly without compunction. As soon as you walk in the cell, the shouts go up from the bunks: let's play for his shirt! Let's have those pants! Before you know it, you have neither shirt nor pants, and the gang is playing cards for your clothing.

curves of the border-to-border rail line were sketched as if it were an ad for international tourism. Every transit point was marked, with indication of how long it took to go from "station" to "station" (via boxcar, of course—the special Gulag express). And northwards from the main route, sometimes with a line and sometimes with a dotted line, went the BAM—

> Way out in Siberia
> the project of the century
> can't be built without the guys
> from the penitentiary.

I do not know whether there are many other cells in Sverdlovsk like number 11. The local prisoners boast that that prison holds from 25,000 to 30,000 inmates at a time. Maybe it does. No official figures are published; they are secret. I can only say what I saw with my own eyes: the prisons are overcrowded, full to overflowing, particularly with young prisoners. We are told by the official media that there has been a drop in the crime rate—then where do they get those thousands and thousands of prisoners who are being transported across the land, from the suburbs of Moscow to the shores of the Pacific Ocean? How many are there, exactly? There is an urgent need for genuinely truthful information, with statistics instead of empty statements that simply benumb the mind. Unfalsified information concerning the crime rate would presumably cause public opinion in our country to wake up; and the increase in juvenile criminality should cause even greater alarm. The view from the inside makes it vividly clear that the system of "education" of people through prisons and camps is a vicious system. These institutions only serve further to corrupt and cripple youth.

But the public cannot hear the voice from inside the prisons, camps and penal colonies. Nor can it see anything from outside: the system is a state secret.

□□□□□

On April 23, 86 men, including myself, were ordered to ship out for Irkutsk. The route, thank God, would be a direct one, bypassing the Novosibirsk transit point. All 86 of us spent the night in the transit reception room, where there was barely space enough for 30 men at the most. I sat crouching against the wall until morning, when they herded us all back again into cell number 11. When the others saw us they all laughed. During the past 24 hours, about 60 people had been shipped out from the cell, but just as many had been added from a new transport, so that the place was just as crowded as it had been before.

I forgot to mention that formalities like issuing mattresses to prisoners are observed in Sverdlovsk with absolute strictness. Any man in the cell who had no room to spread his mattress would throw it on a pile in the middle of the floor. Thus, on the 22nd, I dragged my mattress to the cell; on the 23rd I grabbed the first available one from the pile and turned it back in to the supply room; on the 24th I was issued a mattress again, took it to the cell and threw it on the pile; and on the 25th I carried it out again and turned it in. I spent that night huddled once more in the transit room, and finally on the 26th the transport got going—to the Novosibirsk transit point.

If I had been a free man and in the state I was in, I would have gone to bed and stayed there. And would not have had the strength to get up. But when a man finds himself in Gulag territory he gets a burst of energy he did not know he had. He shuffles along, he walks, he runs, he stands for hours on end, he hangs suspended while others push and shove against him. There is nowhere to go. "The Party says —you must! The Komsomol answers—yes, sir!"

April 27-May 21. I thought as much. If I don't get where I am going by the holidays I will be stuck for a good two weeks. Prison transports are interrupted a few days before holidays; I would be caught in two in a row—May First and Victory Day. I spent both of those days almost in my home region: it is a four-hour train ride from Novosibirsk to Barabinsk. A fellow from Barabinsk in my cell treated me to sausage and pickles out of his food package from home. I took the risk of eating the treat, although I was worried about my stomach. It seems to have been all right; evidently I no longer needed to worry about my digestion: it had not been affected by the hunger strike. As for the rest of my condition— time would tell.

I was in Novosibirsk when the anniversary amnesty was announced. This was the second amnesty to be proclaimed since my arrest: the first was the "chemical" amnesty. The "women's" amnesty came later, when I was already in Irkutsk—the occasion for that being International Women's Year. Naturally, none of these amnesties affected me: I am not a woman; I did not fight in the war; and, furthermore, this was my fifth sentence. But no political offender will be amnestied, neither veterans nor women. Both the five-year-old son of Nadya Svetlichnaya[7] and the daughter of Irina Kalynets[8] will have to wait and wait to see their mamas.

□□□□□

At the Irkutsk transit point I got involved first thing in another incident, although I was not looking for trouble. After standing up for several hours in a stuffy transit compartment, one of my fellow prisoners fell to the ground. Maybe he fainted from the bad air; maybe he was in pain. In the boxcar he had already had an attack of radiculitis. Sensing that I, too, might pass out any minute, I made my way to the door and began to kick it. A guard appeared: "If I take you out of there, you'll be sorry!"

Go ahead and take me, to hell with you, it can't be any worse than this. And I started to kick the door again, right in his face. He went away and came back with the duty officer. "Come on out! What are you cuttin up for? You want the punishment cell? We won't ship you out of here...." And more to that effect.

But when I told him that a man in transit reception had passed out, the captain looked through the peephole and gave the order to take the sick man to the medical section, and to put half of the others into a different compartment. I saw the guard open the next compartment—surprise, surprise! It was totally empty! Maybe there were others just like it off that corridor. And yet they kept us for hours like sardines in a can.

The sick man got an injection and then was put back in with us. He, too, was on his way into exile—an alimony case. We were in prison together at Irkutsk, we were on the transport together to Chuna, and together we were kicked out of the militia station at Chuna with orders to get ourselves fixed up with a job immediately. About three months later I met him on the street in Chuna. He seemed to be almost at a loss: "My exile is over," he said. "I was given disability status, and that means the end of my sentence."

My sentence was only beginning.

□□□□□

In the Chuna militia station, on the commandant's desk, I saw the individual travel order form that was attached to the packet containing my file. Printed in capital letters on the top of the form was the notation: SUICIDAL TENDENCIES.

Not true! The thought never entered my mind to kill myself. So what was the reason for that inscription? Perhaps it was intended as a justification in the event that I should die in transit as a consequence of my hunger strike: obviously he drove himself to it, they would say.

Two red lines were drawn diagonally across the form. This was a familiar indication carried over from my old camp dossier. It meant: ESCAPE TENDENCIES. What will they think of next! A prisoner who maintains a hunger strike for nearly two months must be closely watched, as he displays "tendencies to try to escape." Yet there was not a single mention of the hunger strike in the form.

Escorting us out of the militia station into the street— no place to sleep? Go find a place; no money? You'll get along somehow—the commandant gave us a piece of advice for the road: "See that you get jobs and be quick about it!"

But my job assignment was already waiting for me. I was being sent back to the lumber combine. In 1970 I had served my parole sentence at the same place, and had many acquaintances there. My job was to consist in handpassing a raw six-meter log to the saw. Not every healthy man can cope with that. It would be nothing new to me: in the Perm camps, the foreman had orders to use Marchenko on the heavy tasks. When I got to the lumber combine area, my old friends did not recognize me. Looking at the black beard I had grown while in transit, they wondered where I came from. From a camp? From a hospital? From the world of the dead?

CONCLUSION

If anyone should ask me for advice as to whether he should declare a hunger strike, my reply would be: "Don't do it." In principle I am opposed to hunger strikes as well as to self-inflicted torture in any form. My attitude in this respect is not due to my personal experience in March and April 1975. I came to that conclusion earlier. I was against hunger-striking before, during and after my own hunger strike. Personal experience merely confirmed that attitude in terms of direct sensation as well as of knowledge of the consequences of this pernicious practice. Half a year later I still felt like an invalid, unable to work (though this was not recognized by the doctors at my place of exile), and I have fears that I will be in this state for the rest of my life.

Nonetheless I cannot condemn myself for having gone on hunger strike and maintained it for so long under the influence of my emotion. And what is more, I do not guarantee that I would not do the same thing again in a given situation. When they have you by the throat your feeling of helpless protest may drive you to any extremes. Equally powerful may be your sense of compassion toward another person or persons who are driven to despair.

Political hunger strikes have become a mass phenomenon in the USSR. The news of their occurrence (though not all of them!) breaks through barbed wire and prison wall. But unfortunately the volume of such news provokes an increasingly skeptical reaction on the part of the public. People apprehend facts while forgetting about their causes; and they are unable to imagine the consequences.

The cause of the hunger strike is an extreme degree of cruelty and inhumanity, an absence of legality, and an arbitrary regime.

The consequences of the hunger strike are damage to health and a threat to life. I began my strike on the day of my arrest and followed through for almost two months. A month after I ended the strike I was back to normal living conditions, and yet my health was undermined. Valentin Moroz was on hunger strike for close to five months; he began his strike after he had been in prison for three years, and he terminated it while still in prison—and he is still there now [1975].[9] Ivan Svetlichny,[10] as an invalid, kept up a hunger strike under prison camp conditions for a long time, as did other political prisoners in the Perm area camps. Female political prisoners in the Mordovian Republic went on hunger strike several times. By way of physical rehabilitation they were thrown into punishment cells and into disciplinary barracks (BUR, *barak unilennogo rezhima*).

Remember this: the hunger strike may be over, but the life of the striker is in danger.

Remember: a political hunger strike bears witness to the criminal attitude on the part of Soviet authorities toward the rights and the very lives of their citizens.

I am not about to give advice to anybody. But it seems to me that it is the duty of every decent person, every citizen of the USSR, to call attention to the conditions and circumstances which drive his compatriots to such extremes as the hunger strike.

It seems to me that international cooperation with the Soviet regime in the cultural and economic realms only serves to encourage further cruelty and despotism on the part of that regime as long as no active influence is exercised on the manner in which the regime deals with its own citizens. The existence of political prisoners inside the country—and, to an even greater degree, the tragic situation in which they now find themselves—is no longer an internal affair of that country. Contacts with cruel dictatorships lower the moral level of all humanity. Moreover, these qualities—cruelty, inhumanity and the rule of force—tend to spread through the whole world.

October 10, 1975

poselok Chuna
Irkutskaya *oblast*

Pasha Marchenko

1. Alexander Ginzburg had been placed under Administrative surveillance in April 1974. For several months he was harassed, much in the way Marchenko was harassed. In May he was brought to court for violating the surveillance, but the Judge did not fine him.

2. In Russian, the word "syshchik" can mean "detective" or "police spy."

3. The initials for the Ministry of Internal Affairs, which is charged with the running of penal institutions.

4. Uke or Ukrainian.

5. Her full name is Tatyana Sergeevna Khodorovich, a well-known activist in the human rights movement. In 1974, she and two others assumed responsibility—publicly—for distributing the *Chronicle of Current Events* after nearly two years of suspended publication.

6. An immense construction project, the forging of a railroad across Siberia to the Soviet Far East.

7. A Ukrainian activist who defended the rights of her national culture. She was arrested in the spring of 1972.

8. Kalynets, better known by her maiden name of Stasiv, is another woman activist. She worked as a poetess, but was arrested in January 1972. Both she and Svetlichnaya served their sentences in labor colonies in Mordovia.

9. Valentin Moroz is one of the most famous of the Ukrainian dissidents. After spending many years in Vladimir Prison, he began a long term in a labor camp. In 1979, he was sent to the United States in the celebrated exchange for two Soviet spies. He is the author of *Report from the Beria Reserve*.

10. Svetlichny, the brother of Nadya, is a literary scholar from Kiev. He was arrested in Jaury 1972 and sentenced to seven years deprivation of freedom and five years of exile.

Larisa Bogoraz in Chuna

APPENDIX

The house in Chuna

1. THE CASE OF ANATOLY MARCHENKO

Anatoly Marchenko, author of *My Testimony*, was arrested on February 26 and charged with violation of administrative surveillance. On March 31 Marchenko was sentenced by a court in Kaluga to four years exile. Chuna, Irkutsk Oblast, was later designated as his place of exile.

The following report on Marchenko's case is translated from *A Chronicle of Current Events*, No. 35:

1958. Anatoly Marchenko, a twenty-year-old drilling foreman, is convicted of having taken part in a brawl and sentenced to eight years' deprivation of freedom. (Case reviewed later, and sentence reduced to two years.)

1959. He escapes from a Karaganda Corrective Labor Camp.

1960. For an attempt to cross the border, he is sentenced to six years for "treason."

1960-66. The camps of Mordovia. Vladimir Prison.

1967. Marchenko writes the book, *My Testimony*.

December. For the first time, it is suggested to Marchenko that he leave the country. A KGB agent named Medvedev says: "We'll let you go to any country." The same agent: "We're going to convict you, but not for your book."

1968. Open letter to A. Chakovsky on the situation in camps for political prisoners. Open letters on the same subject to the Soviet Red Cross and to writers.

July 26. Letter on the threat of an invasion of Czechoslovakia.

July 29. Arrested on charge of violating the internal passport regulations. Sentenced to one year of imprisonment (CCE 3).

1969. Two months before his term is up, proceedings are instituted against Marchenko under Article 190-1 (slander defaming the Soviet system of the RSFSR Criminal Code. He is sentenced to two years (CCE 10).

1971. July. Released. Sent to the settlement of Chuna, Irkutsk Oblast, to live under police supervision.

1973. August. Open letter to the UN about the camp case of Amalrik (CCE 30). Open letter to Willy Brandt on detente.

November. Search of Marchenko's home in Tarusa in connection with "Case No. 24." Marchenko's rough-draft diary notes are seized (CCE 30).

December. Marchenko gets advice originating from the KGB: "He'd better leave the country; otherwise things will go worse for him."

1974. January. Marchenko is given a warning at a KGB office in Moscow.

February. Marchenko signs the Moscow Appeal (CCE 32).

May. The Tarusa police put Marchenko under administrative surveillance for one year (CCE 32).

July 2-7. Marchenko joins Academician Sakharov's hunger strike (CCE 32).

Late August. The surveillance is made more harsh, and takes on a deliberately humiliating character.

October 11. After another refusal by the police to allow him to go to Moscow (to bring back his sick son), Marchenko states that henceforth he will consider himself free of surveillance.

November-December. Marchenko is twice fined by the courts for violating surveillance (once on the basis of false information from the police).

December 10. Statement to Podgorny declaring he is renouncing his Soviet citizenship and intends to emigrate to the U.S. (CCE 34). In late December Marchenko is summoned to the Visa Office (OVIR) of the Administration of Internal Affairs, Kaluga Oblast, where it is suggested to him that he leave the country on the basis of an invitation to

Israel. "If you insist on going to the U.S., you'll end up being convicted for violation of surveillance."

1975. January 4. In Moscow the precinct policeman Trubitsyn finds Marchenko at the apartment of his wife, Larisa Bogoraz. She is fined for violating the internal passport regulations, and threatened with expulsion from Moscow.

January 13. Volodin, Chief of the Tarusa Police Force, informs Marchenko that criminal proceedings are being instituted against him (violation of surveillance, Art. 198-2 of the RSFSR Criminal Code). Restraint pending trial: the signing of an undertaking not to leave the city. At the interrogation of Larisa Bogoraz, Volodin expresses doubt as to Marchenko's mental health and states that an order has been made out for a psychiatric examination. (This subject is not brought up again). Volodin also recommends taking advantage of invitations from Israel: "Your husband will be convicted. Everything is in your hands."

February. The Kaluga OVIR begins to press Marchenko to submit the documents for his emigration.

February 25. Marchenko supplies the lacking documents.

February 26. A search of Marchenko's home in Tarusa in connection with the case involving violation of surveillance. Marchenko's rough drafts and other notes are again seized, together with manuscripts, belonging to Larisa Bogoraz. The investigator, Dezhurnaya, does not leave a protocol of the search. Later she says that all the documents were sent to the KGB and none was made a part of the file on the surveillance case.

That same evening Marchenko is arrested and sent to the Kaluga Investigation Prison. *At the time of his arrest, Marchenko declares an indefinite hunger strike.* He refuses to be a party to the investigation. His reason: "I'll be convicted under Article 198-2 not for violating surveillance but for social activism and my intention to emigrate to the U.S."

March 31. Kaluga. People's Municipal Court.

Judge: Levteyev, President of the Kaluga Municipal People's Court. Open court. Present are some twenty of Marchenko's relatives and friends from Moscow and Tarusa, plus a few chance visitors. The bailiff's only demand is that handbags and briefcases not be brought into the courtroom.

Marchenko is led in by guards. He looks bad. His face looks tired and worn, and his lips are dry and chapped. His hands are handcuffed behind his back. At the defendants' bench he falters, and the guards hold him up.

His hunger strike is in its fifth week. Once beyond the partition, they take off his handcuffs. With a wry smile, Marchenko says: "This is how they handle the likes of us now."

He is wearing a heavy sweater. It is plain that he is shivering.

The lawyer Gribkov is present, evidently having been called in by the court. The court refuses a request by Marchenko and his wife to let her take part in the proceedings as a defender. "Counselor Gribkov is here, and the defendant can avail himself of his services." Marchenko categorically rejects Gribkov, but the court appoints him defense counsel. Marchenko refuses to take part in the proceedings, since the court is crudely violating his right to defense. They have foisted an official defense counsel on him, they have deprived him of the right to defend himself and have taken away all the case materials. "They even took the indictment away from me."

> *Judge:* In the record there is a receipt showing that you were given a copy of the indictment.
> *M:* But they took it away before I was brought into court. As you can see, I have nothing with me!
> *Judge:* That's your business.
> *M:* I reserve the right to make a final plea.

The judge, addressing Marchenko in a tone of contempt and distaste, goes through the procedural requirements. Each time Marchenko repeats that he has been deprived of the possibility of defending himself. The court pays no attention to this.

During the recess, Larisa Bogoraz and Natalya Kravchenko request that Gribkov call them as witnesses. They want to tell the court that Marchenko was at home on November 7. The same request is made by I. A. Bogoraz. The advocate rejects the requests. "The defendant has rejected my services." "But you were appointed by the court. You have undertaken his defense..." "Let the defendant himself ask me to call you." "But you are obliged to make use of all information favoring the defendant." "Let him ask me himself."

Nonetheless, Gribkov later accedes to these requests.

The indictment is read: Marchenko has been repeatedly convicted; he has not reformed; he has no regular job; he has maintained an anti-Soviet life style. He has been warned of this repeatedly. In May 1974 the police suggested that he get a job within a month. In that same month he was placed under surveillance for one year. He maliciously violated the surveillance restrictions: in October-November 1974 alone, he committed nine violations with the aim of evading surveillance. During that period he was twice fined by courts for violating surveillance: on November 7 he was not at home after 8:00 P.M.; and on November 25 he did not show up for registration. On December 9 he again failed to register. These three violations served as the basis for instituting proceedings. He gave no testimony during the preliminary investigation, but his guilt was confirmed by witnesses.

The court questions the witnesses. Kuzikov, a Tarusa policeman, testifies that on November 7 he saw Marchenko getting into a bus going from Tarusa to Serpukhov. In order to confirm the violation, Kuzikov and two other policemen went to Marchenko's home. When they rang the bell, a male voice answered from behind the door: "The police have no business here." The policemen left.

Judge: Do you know Marchenko's voice? Was that his voice?

Kuzinkov: I know his voice. It wasn't Marchenko. The policeman Fomenkov, who had accompanied Kuzikov, confirms his testimony. The policeman Arkhipov states that on November 25, Marchenko did not register with the police.

L. N. Starukhina, chief of the municipal gas services (where Marchenko was last employed), gives the defendant a good character reference; he never refused to do any kind of work, and he worked well.

She is questioned as to her conversation with Marchenko on November 6. She says she had intended to assign Marchenko to duty on November 7 and asked him about his plans. He answered vaguely ("Maybe I'll go to Moscow, or maybe we'll be having guests.") But he didn't object to being on duty: "When you have to be on duty, you have to be on duty."

Trubitsyn, the precinct policeman from Moscow, alleges that he saw Marchenko in Moscow on the 7th, 8th, and 9th: alone, with his wife, and with their child. Trubitsyn embellishes his testimony with fantastic details. Marchenko's neighbor, Dmitry Cheremninov, testifies that at 11 A. M. on November 7 he invited Marchenko to his home, but the latter declined, since he himself had guests—his wife's relatives. They did not see each other again later that day, nor did they for the next few days.

Conversations in the hallway during the break: "It's impossible to sit here and watch this! A defenseless person is being beaten..."

"It's not a trial, it's a reprisal."

"Listen. Maybe we should all get up and leave as a sign of protest."

"But Tolya?"

An unidentified inhabitant of Kaluga: "What are they trying him for? There are two cars below, one of them full of detectives. Nothing like this ever happened here before."

Some individuals in plain clothes, without producing identification, try to take one spectator away. They demand that he show them what is in his pockets.

The witness Kuzikov to the witness Trubitsyn: "We should have swigged some vodka and our speech would have gone even better."

Sakharov and Vera Lashkova try to send water to Marchenko. The guards and the bailiff won't allow it: "Let him ask us—we'll give it to him."

Sakharov explains to the bailiff that a person on hunger strike always has a dry mouth. "It's not allowed."

After the recess the bailiff gives Marchenko back the documents that had been taken from him in prison. The judge lets Marchenko address the court. (Plainly, Marchenko believes he is being allowed to make his final plea.)

MARCHENKO'S SPEECH

Marchenko: In the indictment there are references to my anti-social activity; the case record contains material having no bearing on surveillance. Among those materials are the transcripts of foreign radio broadcasts. Other papers taken from me during searches made by the KGB include rough drafts of mine, which the KGB "publicists" have categorized as of possible use in writing anti-Soviet works. After the search conducted back in January 1974, I was summoned to a KGB office and was read a so-called warning which may figure in this case as an aggravating circumstance...

Judge: Please confine yourself to the matters in the indictment.

M: I am speaking to the point: all this is in the case record and in the indictment. The anti-Soviet activity about which I was warned by the KGB is *My Testimony* and other things I have published in the West dealing with the situation of political prisoners, who are brazenly called criminals here.

I have spent quite a few years among political prisoners, and have seen artists, writers, and scientists compelled to do unskilled labor.

Judge: The court is giving you a second warning. Don't take advantage of your situation to insult the Soviet regime.

M: I appealed not only to the West but to the Soviet public. I appealed to the Soviet Red Cross. They answered me: "That's the way it has been, and that's the way it will be." That's how our public men answered me. But my activity was antisocial. I was speaking out for people living under inhuman conditions who had no opportunity to speak out for themselves.

Then, after 1971, my anti-social activity consisted of signing letters in defense of Vladimir Bukovsky and Leonid Plyushch, and my letter in defense of Andrei Amalrik. That, and nothing else, is what was held up to me as anti-social activity.

I come now to the surveillance itself. The indictment affirms that I was placed under surveillance because of my character reference from a corrective institution: "He has not reformed." The decree says that a person may be placed under surveillance only if, as a prisoner, he committed repeated violations of the regulations. I had no recorded violations in camp. Or rather, I had only one; and that one was crossed off the record when I was released. Two weeks before my term was up the disciplinary officer told me that I had no recorded violations of regulations, and I would not be placed under surveillance. Yet a couple of days later I was taken out of the camp and put into solitary. And on the day of my release I was taken to a room where there were some men in plain clothes and I was told I was being released under surveillance. They took me under guard to Chuna, and placed me under surveillance. At that time I wrote to the Procurator of the Irkutsk Oblast, but all my petitions were left unanswered.

Two years later, in Tarusa, when I was told I was being placed under surveillance, they again cited violations of regulations in camp. There is no character reference from the camp in the case record. At the conclusion of this investigation, I filed a petition that a character reference be requested from the camp. My request was denied. This surveillance, too, was ordered not by the Tarusa police but by the KGB, after the search of November 1973 (the warrant was signed by General Volkov of the KGB; the search was made in connection with Case 24, involving the *Chronicle of Current Events*), and after the warning given me by the KGB in Moscow.

When I was placed under surveillance, it was alleged that I had not worked for a long time. At that time I had not worked for one month and twenty-three days. I had not quit my job, but had been laid off because it was the end of the heating season. (I was a stoker.) Nonetheless, I was warned that I had to find a job. Not, however, before I was placed under surveillance but afterward; so that the surveillance was not the consequence of my not working, but rather the warning was a consequence of the surveillance.

This time I drew up a statement as to the illegality of the surveillance and sent it to the West. I did not complain to the Soviet Procurator's Office, since I had no hopes of any reaction from Soviet agencies.

Although I considered the surveillance illegal, I tried to abide by it. I did not want to come into conflict with the Criminal Code. I did not want to provide grounds on which I could be imprisoned. I was thinking of my family. Therefore I complied with the surveillance and did not violate its regulations. Neither the investigator nor the court has shown any interest in the fact that until October 11 I complied with the conditions of the surveillance, and that I ceased to comply with them only when I was finally convinced of their humiliating character. After the summer, all my requests prompted by a concern for my family had been denied. I asked for permission to meet my mother—who is not only aged but illiterate—at the station in Moscow. I was refused.

To visit my sick child in Moscow: refused. To see my aged mother off: refused. When my son got sick, it was thought he might have scarlet fever, I asked permission to take him to Moscow, since at the time there was no pediatrician in Tarusa. For four days Volodin, the police chief, gave me the run-around: "Come back tomorrow: Come back after lunch." Finally, on the fourth day, he told me bluntly that he had not received an answer. Who, I wonder, was supposed to answer that kind of request? After all, the law states that surveillance is carried out by the regular police. I went back once more. The deputy chief told me my request had been denied. Then I told him I would refuse to comply with the surveillance, and took my wife and sick child to Moscow. After that outrageous incident I considered myself free from surveillance. I issued a statement saying that I had been outlawed in my own country. I addressed that statement to the world public. It is hard enough for one person to oppose a gang of bandits, but it is even harder to defend oneself against gangsters calling themselves the state. I do not repent of what I did. I love freedom. But if I am living in a state where concern for one's family and relatives, or love for and devotion to one's child, are criminal, I prefer a prison cell. Where else would I be tried for such acts? I was put in a situation where I had to choose: to renounce my family, or to become a criminal.

Judge: (interrupts Marchenko).

M: In my place the so-called disciplined Soviet man, when he had been refused, would go home, most likely get drunk, and swear at the Soviet regime. But he would comply with the prohibition. Obviously they are trying to make me into that kind of Soviet man (Marchenko points to the witness Trubitsyn)—a doormat with which you can do anything you want. But I have declined such a dubious title. On December 10 I sent Podgorny a statement renouncing my Soviet citizenship.

Of course that decision represents a capitulation to the

all-powerful KGB. More than a year ago the KGB suggested that I leave the country, saying that things would go worse for me if I didn't.

Judge: (interrupts again).

M: Then I decided to emigrate to the U.S. I was told that if I insisted on emigrating to the U.S., I would be imprisoned; that I should go via Israel. This trial is simply the realization of that threat.

I would prefer not to dwell upon the episode of November 7. After I had decided, in October, that I didn't intend to comply with the surveillance, I disregarded its regulations. I am discussing that episode only to show how the police fabricated this case.

So. On November 7 I was at home. We had guests from Moscow—in particular, my wife's relatives, and Natalya Kravchenko. A little after eight Kuzikov rang the doorbell. I opened the door a bit, leaving the chain on, and asked, "Who is it?" Kuzikov said, "Don't worry, Anatoly Tikhonovich. It's the police." I answered, "The police have no business here," and slammed the door. Kuzikov now testifies that he saw me leaving Tarusa. But then why didn't he come and make sure? In October, when I was taking my family back, he wasn't too lazy to get into his car and chase the bus all the way to Serpukhov. But on a holiday, when people like me are in general not allowed to leave their place of residence, he for some reason settled for what he saw, and allegedly let me leave.

Trubitsyn is brazenly lying. Not only did I never go into such explanations with him, I never once talked to him, and never even greeted him. Why didn't the investigator question my wife's Moscow neighbors? After all, it's impossible not to notice a family with a child in a communal apartment where everyone shares the kitchen, the toilet, the bathroom, and the entrance hall.

On the eighth we were visited by our Tarusa friends, the Ottens, but nobody bothered to question them, either.

When I was fined, I didn't hear—and didn't want to hear

—what it was for. Later, my wife found out. At the time—that was still in December—she appealed to the procurator in connection with that episode. But not a single one of the witnesses was called. Is this a trial? It's a reprisal.

Marchenko sits down. The spectators applaud his speech.

Defense counsel asks if he can call the witnesses Larisa Bogoraz, I. A. Bogoraz, and Natalya Kravchenko. The court refuses on the grounds that these people have been in the courtroom.

When Marchenko is allowed to make his final plea, he is somewhat confused. He makes his final plea while remaining seated, saying that he is not able to stand up any longer.

M: I've said all I have to say. This trial is a reprisal on the part of the KGB—one promised me long ago. However, I'm not sorry for anything. I'm not sorry I was born in this country—that I was born a Russian. But, thinking of the fate of my two-year-old son, I appeal to everyone throughout the world—I ask all who can to help me and my wife and son to leave the USSR.

The court retires to determine the verdict. But a few minutes later the spectators are asked to return to the courtroom.

Judge: We forgot that defense counsel has not yet made his plea. We shall now have the pleadings.

Counselor Gribkov: The defendant has refused to discuss the case with me. But from his remarks here I gathered that he disputes the episode of November 7. We have heard the witnesses' testimony. Kuzikov's testimony does not prove that Marchenko was not at home. Marchenko himself categorically affirms that he was home, and refers to witnesses. It is my opinion that Marchenko was at home. As for the other violations, he does not deny them.

I believe in deciding the question of punishment, you should take into account the fact that the first violation was not proven. You should also take Marchenko's positive qualities into account.

Judge: Defendant Marchenko, do you have anything to add?

Marchenko: I shall continue my hunger strike, insisting on emigration to the U.S.

While the court is considering the verdict, Marchenko's friends come up to Gribkov: "Since you disputed the first violation, you should have demanded an acquittal! You're a lawyer. What's the matter, don't you know the law?"

Gribkov: I did more than I could. I know everything, and you don't understand anything...

The verdict repeats the indictment. The episode of November 7 is regarded as proven, and guilt confirmed by all of the witnesses except Cheremninov. In view of Marchenko's situation (the fact that he has a two-year-old child to support), the court found it possible to apply Article 43 of the RSFSR Criminal Code, and substituted four years' internal exile for the deprivation of freedom prescribed by Article 198-2. Marchenko is to be taken to his place of exile under guard.

After the verdict has been pronounced, Tatyana Khodorovich declares: "As a protest against this unlawful trial, I declare a hunger strike in solidarity with Anatoly Marchenko."

2. THE INVASION OF PRIVACY
by Larisa Bogoraz and Anatoly Marchenko

In this letter we shall not discuss reprisals effected with the assistance of a court, although we have both experienced them. Nor shall we discuss professional blacklisting although one of us, Larisa Bogoraz, has been forever barred from working in her field because of her lack of political reliability. Nor, finally, shall we deal with freedom of movement or the freedom to choose one's place of residence, although one of us, Anatoly Marchenko, was denied the right to live with his wife and child, or even to approach their home, and was exiled to Siberia for violating that prohibition.

What we *shall* discuss is a phenomenon which by Soviet standards is relatively inoffensive and innocuous: the phenomenon of searches, tailing, and bugging. These actions on the part of the authorities do not threaten our lives; but they make them unbearable.

In the course of nine years (since 1968) we have undergone ten searches (not counting the shakedowns in prison and in labor camps that occurred during the same period):

Three searches in August 1968 in Moscow.

A search in 1970 in Siberia.

A search in the fall of 1973 in Tarusa.

A search in the winter of 1975 in Tarusa.

A search in the winter of 1976, on a train.

A search on May 20, 1977, in Siberia.

And two secret searches—one in 1971 in Siberia, and one in 1974 in Tarusa. (For that matter, there may have been more secret searches; but we know for sure of only two.)

What was seized from us in the course of these searches? Personal letters, personal documents, notebooks, shapshots of friends, typewriters, and typewritten documents. The last-named included: UN Conventions (1970), an appeal by

Amnesty International (1977), documents of the Helsinki Watch Group (1977). They also seized xeroxed excerpts from foreign newspapers and magazines (*The Times, Le Monde, The New York Times, Russkaya Mysl,* etc.), books and pamphlets by Solzhenitsyn (1971, 1973), Lev Kopelev (1976), and Sakharov (1977), plus Robert Conquest's *The Great Terror* (1977), the Gospels (1971), and samizdat literature, such as *The Chronicle of Current Events* (1970), open letters, statements, etc. And in addition—invariably, constantly, and inevitably—every single word one had written oneself: diaries, rough drafts, sketches, notes, outlines, working drafts of manuscripts already published (in the West, of course), rough drafts rejected by the author himself, and sketches of works one is merely considering writing.

Let us acknowledge the fact at the outset: we know that some materials seized from us are considered "criminal"; e.g., *The Chronicle of Current Events*, and the novels of Solzhenitsyn. We also know, on the basis of surmise and experience, that such-and-such a person was convicted because he "kept" them. (Incidentally, this can be learned only from the *Chronicle.*) We do not regard this as either just or lawful. But that, as we said, is not the subject of this letter.

They take everything in succession. Before beginning the search "in connection with the Ginzburg case," Lt. Col. Dubyansky proposed: "Hand over all of it yourselves."

(The law requires a request that the "criminal" material be handed over voluntarily; and the lieutenant colonel knows the law by heart.)

"What do you mean, 'everything'? You mean everything having to do with the Ginzburg case?"

"In general, everything that might be of interest to us."

"What, precisely?"

"You know. Works by Solzhenitsyn, for example."

"We don't have any." (And, in fact, we didn't: they had been seized from us previously.) "For that matter, you came to make a search in connection with the Ginzburg case, right?"

"...Or by Sakharov.... Do you have Marchenko's *From Tarusa to Siberia?*"

The lieutenant and the lieutenant colonel rummage through all our possessions: the dirty linen and the baby's crib; a volume of Pushkin on the shelf and the used toilet paper in the outhouse; the potatoes in the cellar and the child's toys. For six hours, eight pairs of feet clomp through our two rooms. Special detectors scan the walls and the grounds.

The lieutenant colonels read letters addressed to us before we read them; they glue their ears to our telephone receiver. (Twice during this period our telephone service was cut off as punishment for having made calls abroad.) Naturally, we share the indignation of American citizens at the CIA's meddling in their personal lives. But, really! It's a laugh to read alarmist letters of a Borovik or a Sturua about "total surveillance," files on disloyal individuals in the US, etc. No doubt the KGB has more than one tome on correspondents Borovik and Sturua themselves. And on us, too.

One of the secret searches involved breaking in a door (1971); the KGB lads were trying to imitate burglars. But they took no money or valuables. What they took was: a snapshot of Petr Grigorenko, a novel by Solzhenitsyn, the Gospels, a typewriter, and (of course) all the manuscripts of Anatoly Marchenko.

Eight of the searches were "lawful"; that is, in our presence, and in accordance with a warrant approved by a procurator. Item: by reason of A. Marchenko's unauthorized absence from Tarusa, a search was made at his home, and manuscripts were seized—in accordance with the law. Item: owing to L. Bogoraz's participation in a demonstration, personal letters of hers were seized in the course of a search at her home. Item: by reason of acquaintanceship with N. Gorbanevskaya and A. Ginzburg, a search was carried out and books, photographs, and personal files were confiscated. Item: "suspected of having been a party to (the then secret)

Case 24:" Item: "suspected of having taken part in a train robbery." And so on. Tomorrow we'll be searched and "legally" robbed on suspicion of having had a hand in the Bucharest earthquake or the drought in the virgin-land area.... The investigator fills out a warrant, and the procurator approves it. In the future, owing to the growth of socialist democracy, will the signature of the Chairman of the Supreme Soviet be required? Will he sign? Of course—what are you talking about? He's signed orders for execution—what's a search warrant to him? But what we're lacking right now is not a signature but the Chairman himself, who has quietly and suddenly vanished. No matter: they'll put another one in his place.

Nonetheless, we must dwell on these things in greater detail. On May 20 we were searched "with a view to finding and seizing documents and articles relevant to Case No. 6 having to do with A.I. Ginzburg." So stated the investigator's warrant, in conformity with the appropriate articles of the Criminal Code. Had Alexander Ginzburg himself perhaps deposed that he had conveyed "documents and articles" to us? Or had some witness so testified? No such thing was communicated to us. Nor could there have been such testimony, since no such thing had happened. And nothing "relevant" was found in our home. But the record of the search listed fifty-two of our things that were seized—documents and books. *That* was what they had come to get. It was simply legalized tyranny properly decked out in formalities. Such, in the Soviet Union, is the inviolability of one's person and the inviolability of one's home.

Since all this is legal, it means that Soviet law provides for the violation of natural human rights. It means that we're talking not about an *instance* but about the *principle* of such violation.

We beg the reader to imagine everyday life under such laws and "national traditions." For example: you hide letters from friends in the wastebasket; but the conscientious investigator retrieves them. You keep your books in a manure barrel, but they are discovered, and a photograph of that "hiding place" is published in the book, *Hirelings of Imperialism*. In your notebook you use nicknames for your acquaintances (otherwise they might be perceived by the Eternally Vigilant Eye). But at the KGB office they somehow gather all these things together, and multiply them, and sum them up, and find out who is "Doctor" and who is "Hedgehog." You make five copies of every page of your writing, and bury one in the ground, hide another in the chimney, another in the well, etc., in the hopes that at least one copy will survive. But no. They retrieve all of them—from the ground, from the chimney, from the well: all of your work of the past few years. You'll never see it again. Never. Never did they institute proceedings against us for keeping "criminal" materials. And never did they return so much as a scrap of the documents they had taken.

We are not "underground" operators, but they compel us to conspiracy. Actually, we would be perfectly willing to defend our manuscripts with physical force, since we are restrained neither by moral principles nor by a respect for the law. But we could have absolutely no hope of succeeding: it is impossible to prevent burglary under the aegis of the law and authority. Together with desperation, this situation provokes in us a feeling of infinite humiliation.

Our son is four years old, and has already experienced four searches. The last time he told us: "I wanted to remind you to hide my books...." Hide his books! It's not the two of us but Soviet law that is teaching our child these things. Six months ago "Uncle Kolya" tried to take away one of his books—a child's version of the Gospels. Our son shouted so that everyone in the railroad car could hear him: "Mamma, don't give him my book!" There were a lot of passengers in the car, and so the book was not seized.

Let's try to be objective. The authorities do not devote this kind of attention to every citizen but only to maybe a hundred, maybe a thousand, maybe ten thousand—who knows? But the number of persons worthy of such attention is increasing along with the number of recalcitrants.... But now, for example, our Siberian acquaintances have come within the KGB's field of vision. At first they were recruited to squeal on us. Now the KGB is trying, by means of black-mail and threats, to break up our friendships. Each time one of them meets with us, that meeting is made a matter of rec-ord—and is perhaps bugged as well.

The leader of the Soviet Union recently stated, "In our country, we do not prohibit 'thinking differently' from the majority." Yes, so far there is no such prohibition. There is not yet any special device that can probe the cerebral cortex and extract from it any ideas that are not stereotypes. But already the food for the brains of Soviet man—books and in-formation generally—must be pasteurized in order to destroy the bacteria of doubt and independence. And the results of his "authorized" thinking—"The mind's cold observations / And the bitter insights of the heart"*—will be added to a thick file kept by the KGB, or perhaps more likely, will simply be destroyed.

May 25, 1977
Chuna, Irkutsk Oblast

---

*A quote from the first stanza of Pushkin's *Eugene Onegin* (Translator).

3. ON THE LIFE OF THE SOVIET WORKERS

Anatoly Marchenko was invited by George Meany to attend the Twelfth Constitutional Convention of the AFL-CIO which met in Los Angeles in December 1977. (See CHR 28, pp. 49-51.) Marchenko sent the following letter to the Convention. Marchenko, a worker whose expose of Soviet labor camps, My Testimony, *was published in 1969, is serving a sentence of internal exile in Chuna, a small town in Siberia.*

I learned that I was invited by you as a guest from foreign broadcasts. I thank you for the invitation. I was not able to accept it, since I did not receive your letter. One of those invited—Vladimir Borisov—did receive his invitation but he was refused an exit visa. He was told that "he did not represent anybody."

Recently some of our citizens visited the U.S. as invitees of the American National Committee of Labor Union Action for Democracy. At first they had some trouble with their U.S. entry visas, but they received Soviet exit visas with no difficulty. Whom do they represent? Metallurgists, schoolteachers, the trade union masses in general? Not at all. They are the eyes, ears, and mouthpiece of our regime.

They told us about the desperate situation of one black woman worker; that American teachers beat their pupils and that some American high school graduates don't know how to read; that there is inadequate industrial safety technology in American mines; and that American workers have a friendly attitude towards the USSR. That was all they derived from a two-week trip through the U.S.

How much does that poor black woman make, and what can she buy for her pay? Are her five children in school, and how does she pay for their medical care? Where, how and in what schools did America train its scientists, who year after year have come away with most of the Nobel prizes? Perhaps they are semi-literate? What is the accident rate at an American mine? There was nothing concrete, only a general and grim picture.

If Semyonova had not visited you as a representative, she might have shared with your teachers the information that in our schools there is also a low level of education—I know more than a few semi-literate people who have recently graduated from our schools. And the miner Gatsenko might have told about the systematic practice we have of not registering on-the-job injuries so as not to spoil the statistics and not to deprive a shop or a team of its bonuses. But our representatives, judging by the newspaper account, did not see a single positive feature in the life of working America, and enriched you with the information that we walk around in shoes and our women use cosmetics.

The reporting of their trip is published in the column "Chronicle of Detente." Apparently this means that now you and we, American and Soviet working people know each other better. But we used to read the same sort of stuff about America thirty years ago in the worst years of the Cold War.

If I could visit America, I would not only demonstrate my shoes, but I would tell you that I paid a fifth of my monthly wage for them. I would tell you what the concept of "general employment" means to us, and what, other than cosmetics, the workers are concerned with. In all this I would base myself on my own recent experience of work at a timber-processing enterprise in the Siberian settlement of Chuna. This experience is typical enough of our system of production and does not contradict official statistics.

It was not your fault or mine that I was unable to visit you. Still, I would like my short statement to be heard at your convention. And so let me tell you about the workers' life in a Siberian settlement, Chuna. Of course, I will not try to describe all aspects of this life; I will touch on three questions only.

The average pay of our workers is approximately at the level of the official average pay in the whole country, that is about 160 rubles per month. How does the worker earn this salary? In the drying section, the sorting and stacking of boards is done by hand. Mostly women are used for this work. The damp boards coming in from the lumber mill measure five meters in length, and 19-20 mm. in thickness. The production quota for each worker, be it a man or a woman, is from 10-17 cubic meters per shift, paid for at the rate of 23-40 kopecks per cubic meter. A worker can make no more than four rubles per shift, or not more than 120 rubles a month (about $170 a month at the official exchange rate. There are one hundred kopecks in a ruble). Added to this is a premium for working in a remote area of twenty percent. If the plan is overfulfilled (more than 400 cubic meters per person per month) a bonus is added. All this barely reaches 160 rubles per month. But this income is not guaranteed. In the first place, because of bad organization of labor the fulfillment of the plan does not at all depend on the worker himself. Secondly, the bonus is awarded only when the monthly plan is met by the whole section or shop, not just by the individual worker. And there are a thousand reasons why the section might not meet its plan, and these also do not depend on the worker. In order to fulfill the plan and receive the bonus, at the end of the month people have to work not the one shift of seven to eight hours, as established by law, but two shifts in a row, even including days off. These extra hours are not registered and no overtime is paid for them. The management of the trade union, together with the plant administration, organizes these illegal extra shifts. This happens because the trade union defends the interests of the state, not of the workers, and plan fulfillment is the chief measure of its work.

I chose not to work additional shifts, and I was fired from the plant for "violation of labor discipline" on the decision of the union and plant committees.

The workers of the drying section work in any weather under an open sky—in winter in temperatures lower than -40. The law states that extra pay, the so-called "cold-weather premium" must be paid under such conditions. But this is not paid to us, with the knowledge and approval of the trade union.

Often the weight of the boards exceeds the maximum weight limit set for women or adolescents. Adolescents are put to work in pairs with adults, that is, on an equal basis with them. I refused to work with an adolescent, and the shop foreman punished me by transferring me to other work.

In the settlement many people come from other regions, for instance, from the Ukraine; a round trip takes them 12 to 14 days. Most of the workers at the plant receive 15 days paid vacation. This means that relatives may not see each other for years.

The whole plant, except for the drying section, works in two shifts. Working these shifts are also women with small children, of whom there are very many at the plant. All the kindergartens and nurseries in Chuna are operated in the day-time only. In order not to leave the children alone, married people arrange to work different shifts, and they see each other only on days off. It is even worse for mothers without husbands: they are forced to leave their small children completely alone at night. An acquaintance of mine tells me that her children (aged seven and ten) don't go to sleep until she returns from the second shift, that is until two o'clock in the morning.

Women go to work under such conditions because a family cannot live on one average salary. (Incidentally, our statistics are silent about the minimum wages necessary to live in the Soviet Union.)

Can a family live on 160 rubles per month? The following things can be bought for this sum of money: one and a half decent suits; one third of a black-and-white television set;

one round trip ticket from Chuna to Moscow by air; two tires for the compact car 'Moskvich'; or three to five children's coats.

A kilogram (2.2 pounds) of meat in the store costs two rubles; a kilogram of dried fruit—1.60; milk—28 kopecks per litre (one quart); eggs—.90 to 1.30 rubles for ten; butter—3.60 rubles per kilogram. But most of the time none of this is available in the stores. If one is able to buy anything privately, one must pay almost twice as much: a kilogram of pork costs four rubles; milk—40 kopecks per litre.

Judging from all this, you can see for yourself how far our average monthly pay goes to cover the minimum needs of the family. We may not have unemployment, but the average pay of a worker here is probably less than your unemployment compensation.

It is said that our rents are the lowest in the world; rent for an apartment is only one eighth or one tenth of an average salary. My friend pays 17 rubles a month for his apartment. He and his wife, two working daughters, and a son, a high school senior, live in a two-room apartment (one: 170 square feet, the second: 130 square feet) with a tiny, hardly passable corridor, a cramped kitchen and a shared bathroom. Their multi-family dwelling has facilities: central heating, an electric stove in the kitchen, hot and cold running water, and indoor plumbing. That is the maximum of conveniences known to us.

About a quarter of the Chuna population lives in houses like this. Half of the two-story, sixteen-apartment buildings have no facilities: common lavatories—cold wooden outhouses in the backyard, water at a street pump, stoves for heating. The rest of the settlement's people live in their own or government owned huts, also without any facilities whatever; often there is not even a water pump, only a manually operated well, several hundred yards from the house. We have no standards by which a dwelling can be condemned as a hovel unfit for habitation. If people live there, it means it must be usable. Such living is guaranteed for us in the 21st

Century also: "In the Tenth Five Year Plan it is planned to create for the use of more than . . . 60% of the population well-equipped housing with heating, water, and plumbing." This is the report of the chairman of the Chuna regional executive committee, G.M. Krivenko, at the eighth session of the regional soviet. (*Kommunistichesky Put* [Communist Way] August 28, 1977). This means that the remaining 40% of the people will go on using outhouses at 40 below zero.

What part of our people is provided even with housing such as this is unknown. In Chuna families wait for years to get an apartment, and meanwhile rent what they can get privately: a summer outside kitchen, a bath, a room or a corner in the owner's room. And the rent here is not just symbolic: for a tiny room of seventy square feet they pay ten rubles; while in Moscow rent for a one-room apartment reaches 50-60 rubles a month.

All our citizens have equal rights, including rights to the amenities of life. But recently I learned from an article written by the First Secretary of the Minsk City Committee of the CPSU, Bartoshevich, that among the equals there are those who are "most equal," who have first claim on amenities. I know this myself in practice. Every day I pass by Shchors Street. On one side of the street there are modern private houses with large windows, with all facilities, and with a telephone. They are inhabited by the regional and factory bosses, and they don't have five square meters living space per person, such as is available to my friend, a driver. The people who live on the opposite side of the street drag sleds with containers to the nearest pump, and each backyard there is decorated by a collective outhouse. Obviously, there were not enough water and sewer pipes to go around.

If anybody from the "most equal" set gets sick, he also gets special medical attention. He will have a bed in a separate ward, and he will receive scarce medicine and food, and not half a ruble a day's worth, as in the case of an ordinary patient.

The "most equals" will know only by hearsay whether there is meat or milk in the stores. Everything they need is delivered to their homes, and there is always enough for them of everything, from food to books.

In this way the principle of pay according to work performed has been transformed into amenities given for service to the state and according to rank in the state hierarchy. Our whole society is riddled with considerations of hierarchy. With permanent shortages of the most necessary goods, this principle is carried to ridiculous extremes. In our settlement there exist several distribution systems in addition to the one for the bosses. Lumberjacks can buy sheepskin jackets; the other residents of the Siberian settlement can buy them only if any remain. Today they brought eggs to the store for the workers constructing the Baikal-Amur railroad. The workers at the plant get canned pressed meat; it is handed out right at the plant, so that outsiders cannot somehow get at it. People living on pensions will get neither eggs nor canned meat.

A quilt jacket can substitute for a sheepskin jacket, but potatoes are no substitute for eggs in a child's diet.

In the women's dormitory on the Baikal-Amur project, the most essential things are lacking: a kitchen table, wall-coverings to prevent the cold from seeping through, a dresser. The girls sleep in blankets without topsheets. Topsheets apparently don't exist in any of the other dormitories either, with a few exceptions.

"We issue them only to exemplary individuals. Those who behave themselves," is the explanation of A.Y. Ostrolutsky, chief of the Housing department.

The preceding quote is from the local newspaper, *Communist Way*, May 7, 1977.

And thus the principle of hierarchical distribution of goods extends to everything: from bedding to cottages equipped with toilet paper.*

---

*Such conditions for the working people of our huge country are possible only because we are totally without rights in our own home. In the USSR the

I can understand those Americans who may be dissatisfied with the political, social, or even economic conditions in their country. I sympathize with their striving for a better life. But when I read the ecstatic reports of your compatriots about my country, I would like to address them with the words of our contemporary song: "If you envy this, you can come and sit next to me." Yes, next to my stove, next to me on a bed without sheets, next to me in the communal outhouse (preferably in the winter time).

I invite as my guests to Chuna Messrs. Mike Davidoff, Gus Hall, and anybody else, together with their families. If they agree, I will file official invitations for them. I also invite any delegate of your convention who is willing to visit me; I ask you to communicate his name to me so that I may prepare an official invitation.

Please accept my greetings to the convention and my best wishes for your successful activities on behalf of American workers and for the continued prosperity of the United States.

December 1, 1977   *Anatoly Marchenko*
    Chuna Settlement, Irkutsk Oblast', 18 Chapayev Street

* * *

For additional information on the AFL-CIO Convention and the invited Soviet guests, see CHR 28, pp. 49-51.

A Soviet worker, Valentin Ivanov, who was also invited to the Convention, has emigrated from the USSR (actually in August 1977). At a recent press conference in New York, Ivanov appealed for support for the independent trade union announced in Moscow on February 1.

---

administration, the labor unions, the organs of power and those of repression are all links in one chain, which has totally fettered our whole people. All organizations, including the church, are under the control of a small group of rulers and are subordinate to them. Let our sixty years experience serve as a warning to other peoples!